DISCARD

D1530021

decking

A PRACTICAL STEP-BY-STEP GUIDE

decking

A PRACTICAL STEP-BY-STEP GUIDE

GRAHAM QUICK • JENNY HENDY

with photographs by NEIL SUTHERLAND

SALAMANDER

This edition published in 2002 by Salamander Books Limited,
8 Blenheim Court, Brewery Road,
London N7 9NY, United Kingdom

© Salamander Books Ltd., 2001, 2002

A member of **Chrysalis** Books plc

ISBN 1 84065 484 8

Printed and bound in Italy

CREDITS

Produced for Salamander books by Walton and Pringle **www.waltonandpringle.com**
Project manager and design Colin Walton
Editor Phil Hunt
Photographer Neil Sutherland
Deck building team Arun Landscapes
Production Phillip Chamberlain
Editorial Director Will Steeds

THE AUTHORS

Graham Quick is a deck builder, landscape gardener and fish farmer who has produced and contributed to books on all three subjects. Graham was a pioneer in introducing decking to the British garden centre trade. He has built many decks of different designs and styles all over the south of England and sells decking materials through his landscape supply centre.

Jenny Hendy is a respected garden writer and author whose books are available internationally. With a lifelong passion for gardening, she has been sharing her knowledge of planting and design for the last fifteen years, through writing, lecturing and TV appearances. She now also runs a successful garden design consultancy.

PHOTOGRAPHER

Neil Sutherland has more than 25 years' experience in a range of photographic fields, including still life, portraiture, reportage, natural history, cookery, landscape and travel. His work has been published in books and magazines worldwide.

CONTENTS

INTRODUCTION
What is a Deck?   10

THE BASICS
Planning your Deck   16
Decking Materials   20
Ready-made Decking   22
Preparing the Site   24
Tools and Techniques   26

THE PROJECTS
Simple Square Deck   30
Angled Deck with Access Panels   34
Split-level Deck   38
Raised-level Deck   42
Freestanding Deck   46
Jetty Deck   50
Advanced Decks   54

DECK EXTRAS
Adding a Bridge   58
Adding Handrails   60
Adding Steps   62
Adding Edging   64
Containers for your Deck   66
Plants for your Deck   68
Water Features   74
Other Features   76
Furniture for your Deck   78
Lighting your Deck   82

HELP
Maintaining your Deck   86
Re-finishing your Deck   88
Suppliers List   90
Acknowledgements   91
Index   92

WHAT IS A DECK?

With the busy lives we all lead, it is becoming increasingly difficult to spend quality time in
the garden. The addition of a deck enhances a garden and reduces the amount of
maintenance needed on it, providing more time to relax and enjoy the space. Quite simply,
a well-designed deck will be a worthy component of any garden.

For centuries people have been creating shelters for pleasure as well as for necessity as protection from the elements. In areas with mild climates, outdoor areas have become living spaces in themselves, acting as an extension of the main house. This has lead to an explosion of designer spaces for the garden, using areas that were previously impractical or unattractive. The deck is merely another room in the garden and as much a feature as the garden pond or lawn. There is a place in almost every garden for a deck, whether it is to be used for cooking, eating, entertaining, bathing or playing. It can be an extension of the lounge for the adults to relax without the children or a safe, dry playroom for the children themselves. Decks make an easy addition to the garden and have no end of uses. In addition, they are quick and simple to construct, and anyone with DIY skills can install one.

Decks can be used as level spaces in the garden with a wide range of uses. They differ from patios in that they are

ABOVE *This beautiful deck makes full use of patterned boarding and decorative balustrades as well as changes in level. It really is the ultimate 'outdoor room', providing the opportunity for dining al fresco and for admiring the stunning view.*
OPPOSITE LEFT *The simplest of decks can be created with decking boards just laid straight onto the ground.*
OPPOSITE RIGHT *Using the same techniques as when making the square deck (see pp.30-33) you can create a woodland walkway.*

made from wood and are raised above the ground, but the essential idea of a levelled space is similar.

Decks are predominantly an extension of the main living areas of relaxation, eating and working. The barbecue becomes the cooker and is often built into an outdoor kitchen area with sinks and water on tap, but usually just a gas barbecue is used. With the use of subtle lighting, a small patio

fireplace and a comfy chair, the deck can become an area of peace and tranquillity after the hustle and bustle of work. Now that hot tubs and spas have become more affordable, the deck offers the perfect place for a relaxing soak. Even a sauna can be incorporated into the deck area.

As with any living space the deck can be split into several levels and have steps leading to other areas, each for its

own separate use – the small deck with the morning sun for breakfast to the larger deck for entertaining friends.

The deck can be used to cut down on the lawn area, thereby reducing time and money spent on maintenance. The greenhouse or garden shed can be put at the end of the deck to allow easy access in poor weather. Decking can be extended around the swimming pool to become the 'beach', more pleasant underfoot than hot paving.

AN ACCESSIBLE PROJECT

The idea behind this book is to encourage you to design and build your own deck without the need to go through garden design school or train as a builder. Even if you have not worked with timber and concrete before, this book will guide you through the necessary steps from the start to the finish of your dream deck. You will learn each step with practical information and confidence to visualize, plan and construct your outdoor living space so that it blends with your garden and lifestyle.

As you look round the larger garden centres and builder's merchants you will discover many decking components and ready-made deck units. Whether you buy ready-made decking or decide to custom-build to your own design, this book will guide you all the way.

OPPOSITE *The perfect patio material, wood has many benefits – cool when the sun is on it and warm to the touch at night. The mellow colouration sets the mood for an informal party.*

DECKING TERMS

All decks are built from the ground up with many key elements connected to produce a strong, lasting structure. The following terms, to be used throughout the book, are explained below.

1 Beams are fixed to the top of posts and support the joists. The larger the beam the greater distance between the posts, but larger posts will be required.

2 Footings support the deck and restrict movement to natural timber expansion and shrinkage. Normally 30cm square and 15cm deep, they are situated on firm, undisturbed soil. Concrete building blocks can be used as an alternative.

3 Joists create the framework for the deck boards to be fixed to. The joists need to be fixed at 40cm centres to prevent the deck from having a bouncy feel to it. The thicker the deck boards the larger the spacing you can have between the joists. Your decking supplier will be able to advise you on this. If in doubt use smaller spacings. Decking is the showpiece of the work. Your deck design and pattern will dictate the joist construction underneath. Deck boards should not be wider than 15cm (150mm) as the wider the wood the more likely it is to cup, warp across the width, and collect water.

4 Ledger boards are joists that are bolted or fixed to the side of a house or building to create a fixing point for the deck. It should be fixed so that the top of the deck is below the door sill to stop rain water entering the house.

5 Noggins Are small spacers used to keep the joists at a set distance. As larger decks can wobble, the noggins also make the deck more rigid.

6 Posts support the deck above the ground and must be of sufficient size to carry the weight of the deck and its load. Minimum size is a 100x100mm post.

CHAPTER ONE

THE BASICS

Planning your Deck   **16**

Decking Materials   **20**

Ready-made Decking   **22**

Preparing the Site   **24**

Tools and Techniques   **26**

PLANNING YOUR DECK

The process of designing a deck, selecting an appropriate site for it and deciding on its final use should take full advantage of what the garden has to offer. The deck should blend in with the home and garden, as well as be able to cater for the family's needs. A well thought-out deck will fit into the site and not look like a bolted-on extra.

The most daunting task for the amateur deck builder is the design process. This can be broken down into a number of categories and surveying the site to find the ideal location for the deck is the first and most important. One way to find the right place is to walk around the garden, pick two or three places to sit in and look at what your view would be if you built the deck in this position. Remember to walk away and look at the deck from the rest of the garden to see how it will fit in with the garden's overall design. As you walk over your decking area think about where people are going to walk and how doors are going to open onto it – there is no point having the table in the way of the door or having to climb over it to get to the garden. These small details will make the deck perfect for your needs.

The deck needs to be appropriate for its intended use and the shape in which it is to fit. As a guide, the deck should be the same size or slightly larger than an equivalent room indoors to allow for garden furniture which is normally larger than the indoor version. Decking areas can be

Rearrange the furniture *Start by trying your furniture in different parts of the area in which you plan to construct your deck. As you are rearranging, ask yourself a number of questions. Can you get out of the door? Is the table big enough?*

Estimate size *Once you have chosen your location it is worth using something to outline the size of the deck to get an idea of size and proportion – it is very easy to make the deck too small! Use planks of timber, hosepipes or string.*

Difficult terrain *The sloping ground makes it difficult to see how high the deck will be when it is raised up to the bottom of the windows. Nonetheless, this is still the best place for the deck. The Eucalyptus tree offers some protection from the neighbours.*

separated by introducing alternative patterns or changes in height or direction; by creating an L- or T-shaped deck. Most important of all is that the deck should be in proportion to the house and surroundings.

A deck can be placed in a shaded spot if it is to be used mainly in the evenings when sun is not a priority, but a daytime deck would be better placed in a sunny or partially shaded position. In areas where the prevailing wind may cause a problem, a fence or hedge will be needed to act as a wind break, but this can be added after the deck has been built.

If you have neighbours close to the decks, it is preferable to construct it in a low position as you would not want to be perched high on a deck above your fence for all to see, and the neighbours probably do not want to see you! If you are planning to build your deck over 60cm from ground level it is recommended that you seek professional help in the design and building of it as important factors such as safety must be considered. You will still have a say in how it will look and what features you require.

A deck should look inviting and a large doorway will encourage people to go onto the deck. A small step may be needed to help the transition to the deck if it is much lower than the floor of the house.

As with any DIY project, concentrate on constructing a quality deck rather than an over-ambitious one that may lead to disaster. There will always be the opportunity to add to the project at a later stage.

ABOVE *When this deck was completed, a table and chairs set was added creating an ideal outdoor dining area. The trellis-backed planter provides shelter.*

SAFETY

• Take care with naked flames such as candles on the deck and don't use charcoal barbeques on or near the deck.

• Don't skimp on proper support for wooden boarding – warping or collapse of the timbers could be extremely dangerous. Ensure that all the timbers are properly nailed/screwed down.

• Provide safety rails for sections of the deck where there is a marked drop to the ground and install hand rails for the safe use of steps. A visibly raised edging board will help to prevent chair legs accidentally slipping off the edge.

• Block off the underneath of the deck – rodents damage wiring and burrowing animals undermine foundations.

• Clearly define steps and changes in level, especially when shallow.

• Ensure that planks are laid perfectly level with no protrusions or wide gaps.

• Check timber for rough patches and sand away splintered sections, especially where children will be using the deck.

• Use grooved planking for extra grip, especially on steps and in a wet climate or on a shady deck prone to algal growth.

• Use rot-resistant timber. It will prevent sudden collapse in years to come! Wood must either have been pressure treated with chemicals (tanalized) or be naturally durable. Regularly apply preservative and check for degradation.

• Periodically use a high-pressure water jet to remove algal build-up.

• Employ the services of a qualified electrician if you are in any doubt about fitting external electrics.

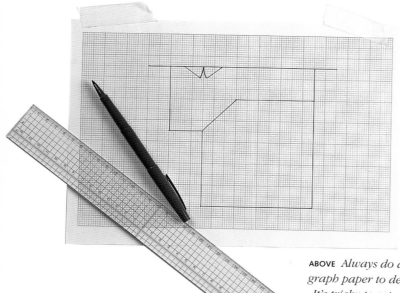

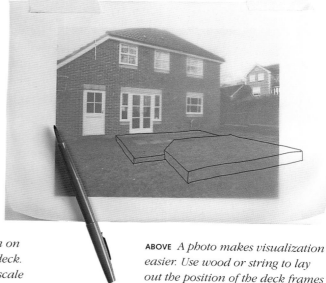

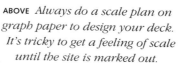

ABOVE *Always do a scale plan on graph paper to design your deck. It's tricky to get a feeling of scale until the site is marked out.*

ABOVE *A photo makes visualization easier. Use wood or string to lay out the position of the deck frames and also view from upstairs.*

DESIGN TIPS

• A deck for dining on should be close to the kitchen.

• A tall fence can provide a screen from sound and wind and offer privacy.

• A deck with shade offers choice for sitting – hot sun or cool shade.

• When planning steps or raised sections in a decking system it is not ideal to step off or up a corner. Cutting the corner off makes for a better transition.

• Steps can be wider than they are indoors to make them more inviting.

• To highlight steps, change the direction of the boards to make them stand out. Grooved boards, running across the step, will make them safer when wet.

• Avoid curved edges and rounded decks as the supporting structure will have to be complex.

CHOOSING BOARD WIDTHS

Whatever width you choose for your boards there are a few factors to consider. One is the span across your joists; narrow timber will only span short spans and this must be decided before you start to build the deck. If you plan to use a diagonal pattern, the spans will be wider and the joists need to be closer together. Avoid boards wider than 6in as they can be prone to warping and drain poorly.

CREATING A PATTERN

The number of patterns that can be created with timber is endless but only a few will look acceptable on any given deck. A few general rules will help you select the right pattern for your deck. Decks with a plain border around them will have a more finished appearance, containing the pattern within.

The smaller the deck, the simpler the pattern should be as complex patterns tend to look untidy and fussy. Complex patterns will make defects in the timber show up much more than simple ones. It is better to spend more money on a superior grade of timber and less on the time and labour needed creating complex patterns.

Long rectangular decks with boards running away from you make the eye follow the boards to the far end, accentuating length. Boards running across the deck are more relaxing and make you want to stay on the deck.

Diagonal boards draw your attention to a view or direct you to steps or a doorway. They can also be used to follow lines from the house or garden.

TYPES OF JOINTS

In most cases the deck boards will be long enough for your deck, but if the deck is longer than a single board it will

LEFT *The finished deck, showing how the change in levels makes it more interesting and overcomes the huge lump of soil in the middle of the wet garden. Also note the angle of the step and the angles of the deck boards to avoid a slip plane.*

be necessary to use additional lengths to complete the run. It may be necessary to install extra joists to accommodate the board lengths, which is something to remember in the building stage.

The three most common joints are:

1. A continuous joint where all the joints run down or across the deck in one line, such as the centre line of a herringbone pattern.

2. Random joints where the joints are at different positions across the deck.

3. Pattern joints where the joints alternate positions but form a pattern across the deck. This is a similar pattern to overlaying bricks in a wall, where the joints are in a basic repeating pattern.

Small decks look best with an intentional pattern – a random joint will look odd and create an uneasy feel on the deck. Large decks can tolerate any of the joints, but a long continuous joint can look very obvious and may become the main feature of the deck – not what you would plan for.

DRAWING PLANS

Drawing up an initial plan will help you visualize the deck and make estimating the materials easier. With a graph pad, go into the garden and measure fixed points such as the house and fence. This will give you an idea of the shape and space available. Another method is to take a photograph of the area and, with tracing paper over the top, draw in the intended design; you can then go back to the measured plan and work out if it will fit in. Once this has been done lay a hose or rope out around the 'deck' and position tables and chairs to make sure everything has enough room to work. You can then finalize the plan and measure up for materials.

THE PAPERWORK

With your plan drawn to scale you can then work out the amount of timber required to make the deck. Start by working out the number of posts needed – it is better to have a few extra than a springy deck. Then work out the number of beams required, if any, and then the joists. Deck board is often sold by the square metre so your supplier will work this out for you. Any extras such as hand rails and spindles can be added to the order at this point. As with any building project allow for an extra 10% of materials to cover damaged timbers or mistakes. It is also important to check whether planning permission is needed, particularly if the deck is likely to be especially large or high.

Tip Try to buy timber that will cover your deck without joints as this will save time and timber. You can often order special sizes to fit your individual requirements. This may cost a little more but the convenience makes it worthwhile. Alternatively, you can design your deck to fit the sizes readily available.

DECKING MATERIALS

In any building project certain factors need to be considered which will affect the look, feel and lifetime of the finished project. The most important one in decking is the timber that you decide to use. There are five factors that require consideration when choosing timber: availability, appearance, life expectancy, structural strength and cost.

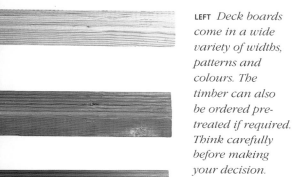

LEFT *Deck boards come in a wide variety of widths, patterns and colours. The timber can also be ordered pre-treated if required. Think carefully before making your decision.*

BELOW *Different types of timber used in the construction of a deck. From left to right: beam, post, 7x2 frame timber, 5x2 frame timber, hand rail, and edge covering strip.*

With the wide variety of timbers you can now purchase it is often difficult to find which wood is best for each application. The majority of timber used in deck building is softwood such as pine. Hardwood is available but the price is often a deciding factor and the finish is not that much better; its resilience to decay is not such a major factor now that timber preservatives are so good. Softwood from colder climates is the best as the growth rings are closer together and give a stronger board, less prone to warping. Some of the most popular woods include Western Redwood (*Sequoia*), which is very resistant to decay and need not be treated prior to use; Cedar (*Thuja plicata*), which is noted for its light weight, great strength and durability;

and Red Pine (*Pinus resinosa*), a timber often sold as Redwood but not quite as robust, though the price tips the balance in its favour.

Always buy tanalized wood if you are using softwood as it is a far better way of resisting decay than trying to paint on a preservative.

When looking for a timber supplier for your deck check to see if they offer a guaranteed life to the timber, often of 15 years or more. If no guarantee is provided move on to another supplier.

The finish on deck boards can be one of many styles. Some have all the sides plained smooth, often available on the best and more expensive types. Others have only one face plained – this reduces the cost and is ideal for those building a deck on a tight budget.

GROOVED OR NOT?

Depending on the look you require, grooved board has a number of benefits over smooth board. For one thing, it is better for steps as the grooves do not become as slippery and channel the water off the decking. Grooved deck boards can also be used to show a change in height or a step by laying them in a different pattern to draw your attention to the change and make the step more obvious.

FIXING METHODS

Fixing the timber is best done with screws as they have obvious advantages over nails. The most important is the 'draw strength' – the amount of energy needed to pull a screw out of the wood is much greater than a nail would require, therefore creating a far stronger joint. Screw joints can be undone easily and moved if required and it is much easier to remove decking boards if you have screwed them down rather than nailed them. Screws will also stop the deck boards splitting when fixing them.

The screws must be corrosion-resistant otherwise they will rust and break over time.

When joining larger joists and posts together, it is essential to use coach bolts as large loads will be transferred to the posts through this fixing.

Your final choice will be how far your budget will stretch to – if you can only budget to pine rather than redwood, then so be it. You will still have a deck that, with the correct treatment, should last 15 years or more.

FIXINGS

Thru Bolts (Rawl Bolts)

Rawl bolts are used to fix the first joist or ledger board to masonry walls. They need to be spaced every 60cm along the ledger to support the weight of the deck and people.

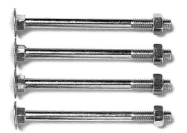

Coach Bolts

Coach bolts are used for joining joists to posts and provide a very strong fixing. Use stainless steel as any corrosion will stain the wood. The length required is the thickness of the two timbers plus 25mm to allow for a washer and nut. Ideally use size M10 or M12.

Coach Screws

As coach bolts except they screw in with a spanner. Very secure fixing which is good for larger timber where the use of an electric drill may be dangerous, i.e. near water.

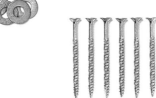

Deck Frame Screws (Pozidriv)

The main fixings for the frame will be 6x80 screws. Secure fixing and easy to undo. Pozidriv are best as they are less prone to slipping when using a power driver.

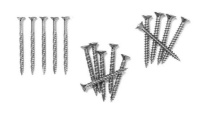

Deck Screws (Posidriv/Square Socket)

The deck boards use 5x50 screws that are self-drilling and self-counter-sinking, making the need for pre-drilling unnecessary. Again they must be corrosion resistant.

Deck Nails

Deck nails are not as good as screws or as secure, but are ideal for inserting noggins because appearance is not important. It is essential to use galvanized nails.

READY-MADE DECKING

As with any ready-to-use products, the cost of decking will reflect the convenience and work already done in the preparation. Providing that additional maintenance is carried out, decking squares will produce an acceptable finish and will last. To avoid unnecessary cutting and rebuilding, the final design should stay within the sizes that the modules come in.

A simple deck can be laid using modular or decking squares. These are ideal for a quick covering over an old patio as they can be laid without a larger and more complex support structure. A simple system of sleepers or battens can be laid and the decking squares screwed directly to them. Because the squares have no structural support they must be laid on a flat, level site. This system is not suited to soils such as clay which expand and contract noticeably – this will move the decking around unless a more heavy duty joist system is installed, in which case it would be better to use a traditional deck boarding instead.

The advantage of the ready-made system is that it can be a temporary patio, moved seasonally or extended

RIGHT *Special trapezium-shaped decking used to make a zig-zag pattern path. With decking, as in other areas, you can have anything made to order to fit in with your garden design.*
FAR RIGHT *Use a row of bricks to break up the expanse of decking and create a 'designer' look that is not only easy to install but also easy to maintain. In addition, if the decking squares are ever damaged they are simple to lift out and replace.*

without any major work to the original patio. If you fancy a new pattern this can be done with little effort and no cutting required. Another plus is the ease of installation – there is no cutting required if it is laying on an existing patio and estimating the number of units required is simple.

Decking squares are perfect for surfacing areas that are difficult to build on, such as on a balcony or small roof

deck, where access for long lengths of timber would be tricky. As with any ready-made goods you are paying for the convenience – it will work out more expensive than a boarded deck, but if you are not too handy with power tools then this is a safe and easy choice. The only limit to ready-made decking tiles is that, due to the thinner wood used in construction, they are not suitable for building raised decks.

ASSEMBLING READY-MADE DECKING

1 *With the area excavated to the correct depth, cover the soil with weed protection mat. If the underlying ground has poor drainage you will need to put down some gravel to improve the drainage situation. Lay out the joists and interlock them as per the manufacturer's instructions.*

2 *As the joists are laid the interlocking system should square-up the deck at the same time. It is important to make sure that all joints are flush as any proud ones will make the decking squares unstable. Once fully assembled check the squares' angles and screw the joists together to secure the base.*

3 *With the base secured, the decking squares can be fitted. The pattern can be created without the need to fix down any squares and moved around until the desired effect is found. They will require four screws per square to fix them down, one at each corner positioned between the surface boards to hide them.*

FAR LEFT *Self-assembly decks surfaced with easy-to-lay square panels can be used to create a stylish patio with a wonderful texture.*

LEFT *When the boards are laid diagonally across the decking squares you can either lay them so that the boards run parallel or for greater effect, rotate them so that they make a pattern of diamonds and squares.*

PREPARING THE SITE

In any project preparation is the key to a quick and efficient job. Once debris has been cleared and weeds have been removed, the deck can be started. Place all the required materials in a position that is easy to reach – this not only makes construction easier but allows for a smoth flow to the work rather than continually stopping and starting.

Although most modern timber is decay resistant, it is best to avoid contact with soil as this will allow moisture to work its way into the deck and spoil the finish. With low level decks some time spent on preparation will help save work in the long run.

The first job is to make sure the ground drains well, as the deck must not sit in water. Measure the deck area out and mark the site with posts. Remove any surface plant growth to 5cm below the ground level and cover the soil with weed block or thick black polythene (perforated every 30cm or so to help drainage) to prevent re-growth of weeds through the decking.

Cover the area with a coarse gravel. This serves two functions: it holds down the ground cover material and allows the joists to touch the ground but not the soil, letting air circulate freely around them. Dig out any live tree stumps as they could regrow and damage the deck.

On higher decks the ground underneath could well be visible and the combination of ground cover and gravel not only stops weeds but also looks neat and tidy.

REUSING AN OLD BASE

An old concrete or paved patio makes a perfect base for a new deck and requires little preparation before work can begin. The patio should fall away from the house to aid drainage. If not, the deck can be bolted to the house and raised to create a slope. If water

Remove plants *Dig out and conserve any plants you want to keep. Skim off annual weed growth or lawn grass with a spade or use a systemic weedkiller to remove perennial weeds.*

Remove loose items *It is much easier to bolt the framework onto a solid surface. It is also far more secure. Removing any old steps like this will also mean that the decking can go straight up to the doors.*

Move pipework *Again it's a pain to cut the decking all over the place. Consider the option of slightly moving fittings if it will make the pipe fit between beams, thereby avoiding having to work around them.*

sits on the existing patio, create a fall on the joists to stop water laying on the timber and soaking in. If the deck is to extend beyond the patio, use piers set on a gravel base to fix the additional decking. If the ground falls away from the deck you will need to build footings to rest the posts on; these will raise the deck to the current level.

WHEN TO BUILD IT

Subject to weather conditions, timing is not really a factor that comes in to play, although obviously spring and summer often give the best weather for construction.

SPACE FOR THE DELIVERY

If the deck is large it is definitely worth getting the supplier to deliver as they with have a properly equipped vehicle to unload the timber. This not only saves time and effort, but also guarantees the safe arrival of the materials.

TIMBER DELIVERY

Due to the weight of timber, find an area to store it that is easy to access; move it once, not two or three times! The position needs to be local to the site and should not obstruct the access of wheelbarrows. Stack the timber with joists on top as you will need them first. Position it off the ground as otherwise water will soak in and make it much heavier to work with; it may even stain the surface. Place a cover over the timber in case of rain.

LEAVE PLENTY OF TIME

Decks are easy to build, but time will pass quicker than you think. Allow twice as long as you predict to build the deck and don't rush it. Never work in dusk or dark conditions as power tools are not safe in this environment. If you can, get a friend to help as it will make the project much more enjoyable than struggling on alone.

SKIP HIRE

There are times when the landscape may have to be levelled and excess soil removed. If this is the case, remove the best topsoil and put it to one side; it can be used in the garden rather than just wasted. The subsoil and any turf can be disposed of. A skip is the easiest method of disposal and it should be kept until the end of the project as any materials left over can be taken away when the deck has been constructed.

Trim plants *Any plants that encroach onto the decking will need to be trimmed away to allow maintenance of the deck. The plants' sap will also stain the timber if it comes into contact with the decking.*

Fix weed block *Fix down landscaping fabric to stop any weeds growing under the deck. This prevents light reaching the soil and inhibits plant growth, but allows water through for drainage.*

Cover grass *It is best to protect the lawn from damage by covering it with a tarpaulin or sheet. This also allows any dropped screws to be collected rather than laying in the grass waiting to be stepped on.*

TOOLS AND TECHNIQUES

Choosing the most appropriate tool for each job is essential in deck building. There is no point in using small, blunt or incorrect tools for a job as this will slow down the work, leave a poor finish to the materials and could actually be dangerous. Power saws, for example, should be able to cut through the largest timber you are going to use in one pass – not two or three. Utilize the right tools and everything will run smoothly.

TOOL HIRE

It is better to hire more expensive tools such as a compound saw (below) and larger masonary drills than purchase them for a single project. When hiring tools, especially power tools, make sure you receive a set of instructions or tuition from the hire shop staff as to the correct way to use the equipment.

Before leaving the shop check that all guards are in place and that all blades are sharp – there is nothing more dangerous than using blunt tools.

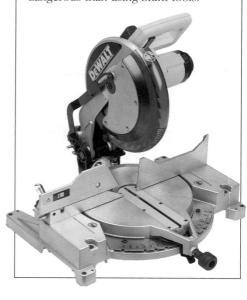

CIRCULAR SAW

ADJUSTABLE
SET SQUARE

SET SQUARE

SCREWDRIVER

SCREWDRIVER
BIT

CORDLESS
SCREWDRIVER/DRILL

CHISEL   HAMMER   BOLSTER
HAMMER

BOLSTER
CHISEL

LONG SPIRIT LEVEL

WOOD DRILL BIT

SAW

MASONRY DRILL BIT

SAFETY

When using tanalized or treated timber you must wear a dust mask and eye protection as the sawdust will contain chemicals from the treatment that are poisonous and should not be inhaled. Make sure any power tools have their guards secured in place.

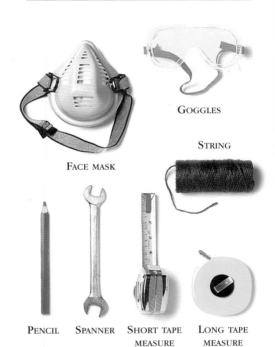

GOGGLES

STRING

FACE MASK

PENCIL   SPANNER   SHORT TAPE   LONG TAPE
                     MEASURE   MEASURE

SHORT SPIRIT LEVEL

MITRE
BLOCK

BASIC TECHNIQUES

Marking at 90° *Very conveniently, the manufacturers of many hand saws now build 90° angles into the handles, making marking out very easy.*

Sawing at 90° *With a sharp saw start to cut at the edge furthest away from you and cut through. Do not let the offcut fall down as it will tear the timber.*

Marking at 45° *As with the 90° cut, the saws also have 45° angles built into them. Mark as before, making sure the angle runs in the right direction.*

Sawing at 45° *Using your thumb as a guide, start where the thinnest end will be and cut across as before. If the offcut tears there is less chance of it showing.*

Cutting a concrete block *Wearing goggles, place the bolster on the block and nick the two edges. Trace along the joining line until the block breaks itself.*

Sealing all cut ends *All cut timber should be painted with a preservative to prevent decay. Use the same solution as the timber has already been treated with.*

CHAPTER TWO

THE PROJECTS

Simple Square Deck **30**

Angled Deck with Access Panels **34**

Split-level Deck **38**

Raised-level Deck **42**

Freestanding Deck **46**

Jetty Deck **50**

Advanced Decks **54**

SIMPLE SQUARE DECK

The most straightforward deck you can build is square or rectangular. Here the timber can be used most effectively and there's only a simple base to build. Working with standard lengths of timber, this deck was created using uncut boards to ease the process of its construction, thereby avoiding unnecessary cutting and wastage.

The old patio sloped towards the house having sunk over the years, so a new patio needed to be installed. However, the work and expense of digging up and removing the old patio was prohibitive, so it was decided that a deck would be built instead.

The deck's main use was to be an extension to the dining room, with access to the deck from a set of double patio doors. With this in mind the basic design was drawn out on tracing paper. The size was decided upon by setting out the table and chairs on the old patio and then marking it out, remembering to leave space for the walkways to and from the patio doors.

After a quick check, the deck was built at 3.6m by 3.6m, which was the length of timber that the decking boards and joists came in. This made for a simple and straightforward construction.

The only difficulty to overcome was the slope back towards the house. A simple solution was to bolt the first joist – the ledger board – to the house, raising the deck to slope away from the house. From a safety standpoint, the deck boards ran across the deck so that when stepping out onto the deck from the house, the grooves reduced the chance of slipping and aided drainage on the surface of the deck.

ABOVE *This before shot shows the patio's problem slope to the house and to the left. This was easy to cure by fitting a deck.*
RIGHT *Such a simple deck requires little maintenance – nothing more than a quick sweep once a week.*
OPPOSITE *The final project completed, with a table and finishing decoration. A quick and easy solution to replacing the old patio.*

1 *Using a tape measure, mark off equal distances for the lag bolt holes. Check to make sure the joist and deck board will be below the doorstep to prevent rainwater from running in.*

2 *When choosing the positions of the bolt holes, avoid the mortar joints – the brickwork will provide a far better fixing. Wood drill through the wood, then use a masonry drill to penetrate the brick.*

3 *Hammer a rawl bolt through the timber and into the wall. Make sure the nut is on before you hammer it home otherwise the thread will be burred over and the nut will not fit.*

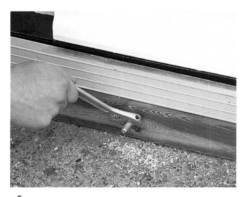

4 *Tighten the nut with an adjustable spanner until the nut starts to be drawn in to the timber and the wood is tight to the wall. Check the level.*

5 *Fix the first joist to the ledger board. It is important to make sure that the top edges of each timber are level with each other.*

6 *The outer joists can be attached with screws, which should be long enough to go through the first timber and into the other by at least 25mm.*

7 *(left) With a builder's square or a large set square line up the last joint and fix with a screw; then check that all the other corners are at 90°. If the deck is square the diagonal measurements will be equal.*

8 *(right) Measure out and fix supporting joists at 40cm centres. Fix from each side by screwing in at an angle. If no edging is to be used this method can be used to hide the screws from view.*

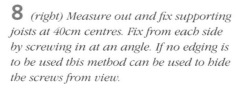

9 *Measure and cut two rows of noggins to stretch across the beams (left). Alternate their position so you can get the nails in. Use screws on the outside of the deck frame and nails on the area hidden by the deck boards. Place the noggins on the ground to provide extra support to the frame (above).*

10 *Screw the first deck board into position. Make sure it is parallel to the first joist as this will set the pattern for the rest of the boards.*

11 *Use a 5mm spacer such as a spanner to set an even distance between each deck board. This will allow room for the timber to expand when it is wet.*

12 *Once the ends of the deck boards have been fixed down the rest of the deck can be screwed down. Use a chalk line to line all the screws up together.*

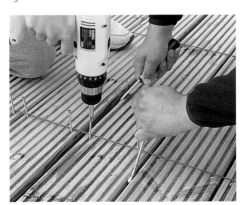

13 *(left) If the deck boards are warped, insert the 5mm spacer between the boards and use a chisel to lever the boards to the correct position. Then screw in the boards.*

14 *(right) To finish the edge screw down a length of board to use as a straight edge. Make sure the distance between the board and the circular saw blade is such that the saw will cut the decking boards flush to the joist. Run the saw along to trim the ends of the deck board to a uniform length.*

ANGLED DECK WITH ACCESS PANELS

This deck is still an easy one to build but has a few more issues that need to be addressed before the work can be started. The position of the deck coincides with a manhole cover, two drains and a drainpipe. Fortunately, these elements are all easy to work into the finished deck and the design is such that they are still readily accessible.

The site here would have required a vast amount of work to create a new patio. The old concrete patio would have to be broken up and removed, and a new base and surface laid, so it was an easy decision to build a deck instead. As the old patio sloped towards the house, the deck would have to be raised at the house end to level the area off and encourage the water to drain away from the house.

The deck's primary use is to cover the old patio, but also to serve as a breakfast deck for two chairs and a small table. As people will be walking out of the door, the grooves need to run across the deck to give extra grip and prevent potential accidents. The only other consideration here is the position of the manhole cover and drains – each must be easy to get to without taking the whole deck apart.

The other difference to the basic deck is that the corner is cut off – a 90° corner does not allow a simple step and stepping off the corner could cause it to splinter. The angled corner draws you to use it as the access onto and off the deck and allows a wide, safe step area. With the basic design drawn out the building can start. Again the full length of board is to be used to cut down on materials and wastage.

ABOVE *This photo shows the shape of the old patio and the drains and manhole that need to be included at the design stage.*
RIGHT *The angled corner provides a safe access point to and from the garden.*
OPPOSITE *The completed deck looks simple yet appealing, providing a perfect base for attractive deck furniture.*

1 *Screw the outside frame together. For the 45° corner, cut one of the timbers at 45° and the other at 90° and then screw the two timbers together.*

2 *If obstacles such as drains are in the way, a box will have to be built around them, not only to protect the grids but also to provide support for the deck boards.*

3 *Add the rest of the timbers. If access is required to large drainpipes, the cut-out needed may be the width of the board so additional framework is not required.*

4 *With all the full length joists installed, the noggins can then be fixed between them. These will stop the deck expanding and warping the joists.*

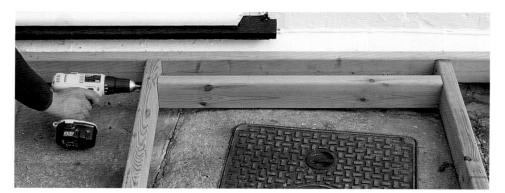

5 *Access to drain covers is essential so joists should not be placed over them, but as close to them as possible. Where a normal timber will not fit around the drain, insert an extra noggin to hold the weight of the boards. Make sure all fixings near drain covers are screwed so they can be easily removed if necessary.*

6 *(left) As this deck over runs on to the lawn, a weed-blocking material is needed to stop the grass growing under the deck. Use large nails to fix it in place. If you want, you can also use washers to stop the nails going right through the fabric.*

7 *(right) Start laying the deck boards from the back and work to the front of the deck. If the board has to be cut around an object such as a drainpipe, use a level to line up the separate lengths.*

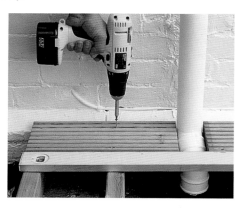

8 *Use a hole saw to make a neat hole for the drainpipe to pass through the decking (inset). It may be necessary to use extra pipe fittings to get the pipe to go through vertically – this saves trying to drill a hole at an angle to suit the pipe. Using the level as a straight edge (right), align the join in the small access panel with the centre of a beam and screw in the deck boards on both sides of the join. Cutting all the odd lengths from one piece of timber ensures that the wood colour and grain match.*

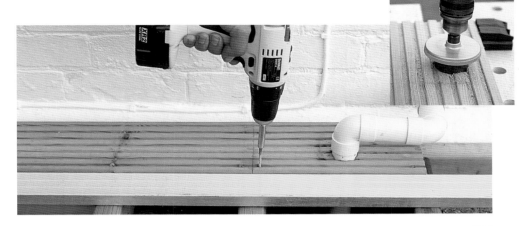

9 *As you reach the manhole cover you will need to cut each board so that the lengths butt-up together in the middle of each supporting timber and so will allow easy access to the drain. Space and fix each one down at the ends and, with a level, match up the board to cover the total length of the deck.*

10 *(above) Overhang the boards with the largest overhangs at one end as this will give you offcuts of a useful length. Fix with two screws at each end and two per joist to stop any cupping. Space evenly as before and fix in the middle of the boards.*

11 *(right) Screw or clamp a straight edge to the deck and run along with a trim saw to create a uniform overhang. Alternatively, if an edge is to be added, trim level with the joist.*

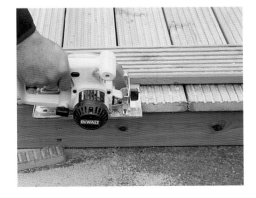

SPLIT-LEVEL DECK

This is a simple deck, combining two decks that overlap each other to create a split level. The different directions of the deck boards on each level show the height difference. The garden was very wet and shady which meant it was out of bounds for most of the year, but the addition of the deck has allowed more use and less maintenance.

The aspect of the garden means it has shade problems and as such is a poor spot to grow even a basic lawn. The first plan was to have a small deck outside the patio doors and a second larger one under the window extending out into the garden.

When at the planning stage it was noticed that the second deck would have been fixed above the damp coarse, this was deemed unacceptable as it could encourage damp into the walls. In the final design a longer low deck was positioned up against the house below the damp coarse, which alleviated the gap that would have been left between the house and the main deck and a step up to a second deck in the garden.

The second deck was to be used for barbecues, so a large low level was incorporated that covered part of the old concrete slab patio and part of the wet garden. In the construction, the posts were placed on a concrete block that kept the timber above ground level and out of the wet soil, thereby reducing the chance of decay. It was important to treat all cut surfaces with preservative to stop water entering in these conditions. As the deck is in a shaded damp position, the surface will need treating regularly to prevent algae from growing on it.

ABOVE *This photograph shows the small, inadequate patio that was present before the deck was built.*
RIGHT *The different deck levels are highlighted by alternating patterns.*
OPPOSITE *The completed deck in use, covering the patio, manhole and part of the garden. The garden now has a useable area for outdoor dining and socializing.*

1 *Measure and cut the timber for the first square. If you have a flat area of ground you can make up the first square of the deck frame, then move it into position and bolt it to the wall.*

2 *(right) With the outer frame completed on the first part of the deck, cover the ground with weed block and complete the first base as before, screwing the joists together at 40cm centres. Take care of the ones near the air brick where the gap is narrower to avoid obstructing it. The second part of the deck can be put together, the outer frame first, and then the two sections screwed together before fixing the other joists, as it will be difficult to get the drill in between them. Any areas of grass need to be covered with more weed block. Then fix the joists in position as before at 40cm centres.*

3 *To prevent the air bricks from being obstructed, cut away any timber that will cover them and add a second length of joist inside to carry the deck board.*

4 *If the deck is going to be above ground level, add posts. Dig a hole and stand the posts on a concrete block to spread the weight. Secure using coach bolts .*

5 *If the joists are over 1.5m in length add noggins to stop them spreading when the deck boards expand in the wet. If the noggins are not visible you can nail them.*

6 *(left) Diagonal boards need to be laid with the use of a square to obtain the correct angle.Using spacers as before, leave a 5mm gap between the wall and the end of the deck board, and 5mm between the boards. Leave extra space when you get to the air brick. Use the square and spacers to place in the correct position.*

7 *(right) After the deck boards have been laid, finish the edging detail by sawing off the excess timber with a circular saw. For any difficult areas use a sharp hand saw. Paint the ends with preservative.*

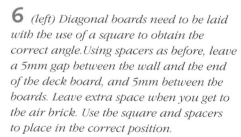

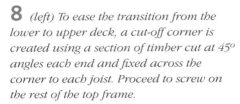

8 *(left) To ease the transition from the lower to upper deck, a cut-off corner is created using a section of timber cut at 45° angles each end and fixed across the corner to each joist. Proceed to screw on the rest of the top frame.*

9 *(right) Where the frame is above a solid concrete base, screw a hole into the post, then knock in, bolt and tighten coach bolts. Remember to seal any cut ends with timber preservative before fixing together.*

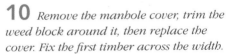

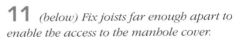

10 *Remove the manhole cover, trim the weed block around it, then replace the cover. Fix the first timber across the width.*

11 *(below) Fix joists far enough apart to enable the access to the manhole cover.*

12 *(above) As you work across the deck cut short boards around the manhole cover and then continue each board to overhang as before. Space the noggins through the centre of the deck to increase the ridgity of the base. Posts can be fixed to both joists to give a more secure joint.*

13 *(right) Using a straight edge as a guide, run the circular saw along to trim off the overhanging deck board and so complete the split-level deck.*

RAISED-LEVEL DECK

On this site the garden sloped away from the house too steeply for a conventional patio to replace the small, 1.3m-wide 'patio' that was in place. When the measurements were taken a difference in height of 70cm was recorded, so we felt that a raised deck would be ideal. As the deck was to be elevated above 60cm, it needed a hand rail for safety.

The basic remit for this deck was to replace a useless patio with an area for dining and relaxing. Situated in semi-shade on the east of the house, the deck needed to extend into an area of the garden that received sun. Proximity to the fence provided another obstacle to overcome, as the deck would raise the owners above the fence into the neighbours' line of view. To help resolve this, the step was removed from the old patio to lower the deck and a large trellis-backed planter was fitted in front of the fence to raise the screening height, offering more privacy for both parties. The sloping ground was easy to accommodate with the deck and since the deck was raised, a hand rail was fitted for safety and a feeling of enclosure.

A number of details were noticed during planning – air bricks for house ventilation and a climbing plant were two elements that needed to be built around. The area was to be covered with a diagonal pattern to add visual interest and to guide people to the step at the front of the deck. Being close to the fence, a gap was left between the deck and fence to provide access for maintenance and repairs. Steps were also fitted to allow access to the passageway behind the deck.

ABOVE *This shows the original patio and the slope of the garden. The small rockery was removed to make way for the deck.*
RIGHT *The deck is now an ideal spot for outdoor eating and entertaining.*
OPPOSITE *With added furniture and props, the space is transformed. Note how the trellis provides a screen for added privacy for neighbours on both sides of the fence.*

1 *Lay out the size and shape required with the joists. Install the posts where needed and cut to correct height using a long level. Leave a gap of 15cm between the deck and the fence for maintenance.*

2 *Cut excess timber away from the air brick to allow circulation. With a level mark the position on the wall. Slide the timber behind the plants to avoiding damaging them.*

3 *With the timber in place secure it by drilling a hole through the joist into a brick, not a mortar joint, and fix with a rawl bolt. Fix at least four bolt diameters from the edge as it will provide a stronger fixing.*

4 *(left) Although the timber is not flush with the post, the coach bolt will easily take the weight. The longer joist needs two bolts.*

5 *(right) On the cutaway corner, place the posts further back to avoid the screws on the front joist and to leave space for supporting joists. Position the angled step, measure and cut wood. Dig holes for two posts and fix corner step with screws to create the finished outline frame (below).*

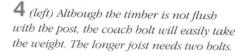
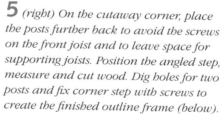

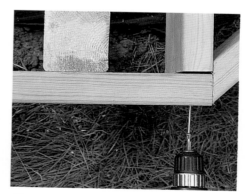

6 *With the set-back post, the extra room for the joist can be used. Be careful to avoid the screws in the front joist. Before the deck is laid, paint any cut surfaces with preservative.*

7 *(left) Lay weed block and fix in position. Measure out and fix all supporting joists.*

8 *(below) Add noggins to the support structure, starting with any that are needed to bypass air bricks and plants. It is best to screw rather than nail these in place. Leave enough space for plants to grow thicker.*

9 *With the rest of the noggins added to the base, start laying the deck boards from the front edge. You can use a block to keep the edge flush with the front of the joist.*

10 *Continue to fix the deck boards as you go across the deck. When you arrive at the air brick leave a larger gap for circulation and space for the plant to grow.*

11 *With the boards screwed at both ends, stretch string across the deck to align with the base timbers. Screw the rest of the boards to the joists, adjusting the gaps as you go.*

12 *(left) With the fence so close to the deck it would be difficult to screw down a deck board as a guide. So pencil along the board to use as a guide line. Saw by hand or use a circular saw if there is space.*

13 *(right) For the other sides of the deck, fix a straight edge down across the deck and use a circular saw to trim off the excess. Set the saw to a depth just a little more than the thickness of the board to give a cleaner cut.*

FREESTANDING DECK

This garden provided a site that was of no use to the owners, sloping away from the rest of the garden. It was in partial shade, was made up of dry soil and a had a fence and wall on two sides. Not even the grass grew well. A freestanding deck was seen as the best way of dealing with all the problems and the slope was levelled off without too much work.

This site provided a good chance to build a freestanding deck away from any other permanent structures as have been used in other projects. The damp coarse in the garage was close to the ground, so raising the soil to level the site was not an option. A sunken area in the corner would also not be appropriate as removing enough soil to allow a level patio area and retaining walls to be built would be a huge undertaking. As the garage wall in the background belonged to the property next door, it would not be possible to attach the deck to it, and access had to be left for maintenance if needed.

The deck's primary use was to be as an attractive and useful section of the garden for sunbathing and relaxing in the evening. With this in mind the deck needed to be large enough for two sun loungers as well as a table. As the deck was in a 'plantless' part of the garden a built-in planter was used to bring a touch of colour into the otherwise dark corner where the fence and wall met. As the corner was featureless, the deck was originally designed in an octagonal shape; a corner left intact on the far side for the planter resulted in the platform ending up with seven sides. The deck boards were laid parallel to the step position, drawing you into the deck.

At the moment the deck is a little stark and exposed but a feeling of enclosure could be achieved by adding a trellis panel planted up with quick growing climbers at an angle to the brick wall, following the edge of the deck.

ABOVE *This image shows how the site sloped to the bottom of the wall and into the corner with the fence.*
RIGHT *Foliage provides a visually pleasing contrast with the colour of the deck timber.*
OPPOSITE *A pair of deckchairs, a table and a parasol complete the transformation.*

1 Lay out the size required for the deck and, using a number of offcuts as markers, place them over each corner. Measure each of the five shorter sides until all are equal in length, then measure the two longer sides.

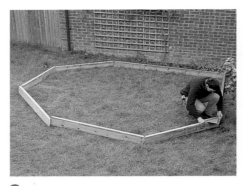

2 When all sides are the correct length mark each for cutting, taking care to measure the outside of the frame. Cut each to size and at a 45° angle. Place the timber in position and check the lengths and angles once again.

3 Check diagonal measurements with a tape before assembly to check for square, because it is important that the sides are parallel. If they are not placed in a parallel position, the deck boards will not run square across the deck.

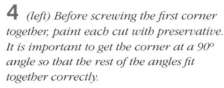

4 (left) Before screwing the first corner together, paint each cut with preservative. It is important to get the corner at a 90° angle so that the rest of the angles fit together correctly.

5 (right) Screw the 45° corners together. Always screw through the angled timber in to the end of the joist. If the wood starts to split, drill a piolet hole through the angled timber, but not through the timber behind.

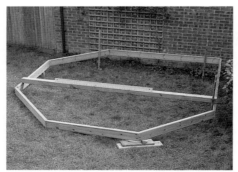

6 Using a measuring tape, check that the position of the deck is parallel to the wall as it will look strange if it is not. Leave a space large enough to get behind to do any maintenance of the deck and of any plants that are growing there.

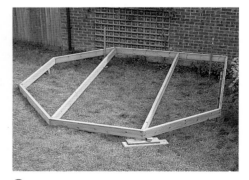

7 The more hands the better for this part. Lift the deck frame up and level it in position; use posts temporarily screwed to the frame and blocks to do this. Check for level with a straight edge and a long builder's level.

8 Fix the first two joists into place across the frame – these will ensure that the frame remains rigid. It is important that you keep checking for level and mark out the position of the posts.

9 *With the two main joists in place, measure up and secure the rest at 40cm centres. To accommodate the angled sections of the outer frame, cut these joist ends at 45°.*

10 *With the support finished, dig out and stand posts in position. Bolt the post to the frame with coach bolts. Check the level and square of the angle. You can use concrete to secure in place, but let the concrete dry overnight before continuing.*

11 *Cover the grass with weed block and fix into position. Install noggins between the joists to add strength. Always start laying the deck boards from the front edge and screw each end down. With a spacer in place, fix down the next board.*

13 *Stretch some string across for a guide. Tap the screws in ready to tighten later. Use the spacer and open/close the boards with a chisel to get an even spacing. Tighten each pair of screws to hold each board down.*

12 *(above) Work across the frame and continue to fix the deck boards down, all the while using the spacer to maintain an even pattern across the deck. Remember to allow enough overhang of the boards for the final edge cut.*

14 *(right) Using a plank of timber as a guide for the circular saw, and with the saw set to cut just thicker than the deck board, trim all around the edge of the deck to finish. Treat all surfaces with preservative as before.*

JETTY DECK

The thought of sitting on a deck with a drink or enjoying a quiet dinner overlooking a tranquil lake or pond is very appealing. It is also relatively easy to construct for anyone who has the garden to accommodate the structure. This deck design is a single level overhanging the water, making use of an area that is otherwise impossible to utilize.

Decking overhanging water may sound like a recipe for disaster but with the correct guidance it should pose no problems at all. The idea here was to create a peaceful dining area away from the house in which to relax and enjoy the view of the pond. The basics of a cantilever deck are quite easy to understand and work out. No more than 25% or a quarter of the length of the deck must overhang the beam, to a maximum of 1m, as the 75% acts as a counterbalance. If the deck joists are 3.6m, the overhang should be no more than 90cm. Heavier grade joists should be used, no less than 150mm by 47mm. A beam is necessary to spread the load from all the joists to the foundations.

In order to keep the deck profile low a larger beam than necessary was used on its side to support the deck. With the basic design undertaken, the deck could be started. If the pond is a man-made one with a liner, be careful not to damage it when digging the foundations out or by dropping tools in the water.

The use of mains-powered electrical tools near water is highly dangerous, so always keep tools well away from the water. Only use cordless tools when working on the deck itself. Safety is of paramount importance.

ABOVE *Before the deck was built this area was untidy and unusable. The banks were slippery and difficult to maintain.*
RIGHT *The deck covers the pond with ease, making a feature out of nothing.*
OPPOSITE *The finished deck with added furniture and containers. The bridge was added at a later stage, to allow easy access on and off the deck.*

1 *Start the deck by building the frame on the ground. Check each timber for defects as the extra load of the jetty could cause a failure. Screw each joist together with three screws for added security.*

2 *Level the frame off and use blocks to hold it in place. Now square the frame by measuring from corner to corner across the longest diagonal – if the deck is square the measurements should be the same.*

3 *On a cantilever deck, the overhang should not exceed more than 25% or 1m of the deck's width, whichever is the smaller figure. Measure back 25% and mark the sites from the piers.*

4 *Dig out a hole for the piers and concrete in place. Check to make sure the piers are level and parallel with the frame otherwise the frame will be out of position.*

5 *Lay the beam across the piers and check the level. Make the distance between the front of the frame and the centre of the beam 25% or less of the deck's total length.*

6 *To hold the beam in place construction adhesive can be used to glue it to the piers. The frame can then be fixed to the beams by screwing it in at an angle.*

7 *(left) With the frame in place, fix all the supporting joists at 40cm centres across the frame. The overhang into the pond means that the loading pressure on this deck will be greater than on a ground deck – because of this it is recommended that 150x47mm joists are used.*

8 *(right) With each end of the joist secured in place, screw each one to the beam, ensuring that the 40cm centres between joists are maintained.*

9 *At the back edge of the deck dig foundations and install posts at the two corners opposite the beam. Mark off the correct height using a level on the frame and cut off the excess.*

10 *With a wood drill, make a hole for the coach bolt to go through and bolt the joist to the post. Repeat further down for security. Make sure you fix the post to the joist that runs out over the pond.*

11 *Concrete the post in and pack the soil back into the hole with a piece of timber for added weight. Paint all surfaces with preservative before fixing the decking boards down.*

12 *(right) Cover the soil underneath the deck with weed block and fix down. Install some noggins in the overhanging part of the support to stop any movement in the joists; with the beam in place there should be no need for any other noggins. As the deck is square the first decking board can be cut at 45° across one end and fixed down to one side of the centre of the corner. Leave the other end overhanging the deck and secure as before. Use cordless screwdrivers when working near the water to prevent any accidents.*

13 *(left) With the use of a 5mm spacer between each board, fix down the next boards and work to the edge. Secure the boards all the way along as you go. This gives a safe position to work from.*

14 *(right) Screw a straight edge down as a guide and run a circular saw along to finish the deck surface, using eye goggles for protection. Treat all cut surfaces with preservative. Be careful not to drop anything in the pond.*

ADVANCED DECKS

It is important to realize that the most expensive does not necessary mean the best. A simple,
well-designed, professionally built deck can often be a better way to spend your money than a
not-so-well-built DIY deck. If for any reason you feel unhappy with a project that is beyond
the methods shown in this book, look to a deck builder to do the work for you.

As with any idea of installing a garden feature, some of us want to build something just a little bigger and more ambitious. In any large-scale building project such as constructing a deck it is best to seek advice about its design and construction as a small mistake could be disastrous and dangerous to people – as well as the building it is attached to.

Planning is even more important when the decks are more complex as rectifying mistakes can be very expensive once construction is underway. If you are going to build the deck in stages to spread the cost, or to allow extra work to be carried out, explain to the builders what sections are to be constructed. This will give them an idea of how to plan the deck in sections that can be easily completed and left in a state that makes the deck not only useable, but structurally safe.

Once the deck's use and position has been decided, a call to the decking company is required to allow them to come out and complete your design to local building regulations, if any apply. Always get two or three quotes to make sure you are getting what you want, and ask to see samples of the timber before they start work.

With a professional company building your deck, you will be able to

ABOVE *This well designed deck has all the right qualities: it is well built, on a good site and has space to be useful.*
LEFT *A different alternative to paving around a pool, cooler and more pleasant to walk on and more attractive.*
OPPOSITE *A good choice of colour has enabled this deck to blend in with the surroundings, without it overpowering the house.*

have almost any type of deck shape or size build that you can imagine.

Multi-level decks from a second floor balcony can be created with a stairway to lower levels for dining and walkways to other areas of the garden such as the spa, hot tub or swimming pool. There is no limit to design or size, providing the deck solves all your requirements for use and is within your budget.

DESIGNING YOUR OWN

You may want to design your own deck and then supply the drawings to the deck builders yourself for them to quote for. Remember to listen to their comments, as some of your ideas may be too complex or just not feasible, so do not ignore what they have to say. If you are sure that the design fits your requirements, get another builder to give you their opinion. If both builders agree that the design is not workable, you will have to think again.

If the deck changes the appearance of the house you will need to check to be sure that planning permission is not required. If it is, any building regulations are applied to the deck and its supporting structure.

CHOOSING A DESIGNER

Before you choose a designer for your deck it is preferable to check out two or three of their previous designs to see if you like what they have done.
A good designer will be able to judge exactly what you require from your existing house and garden. Approach a few different designers and see who produces the best and most workable kind of deck for your needs.

CHAPTER THREE

DECK EXTRAS

Adding a Bridge **58**

Adding Handrails **60**

Adding Steps **62**

Adding Edging **64**

Containers for your Deck **66**

Plants for your Deck **68**

Water Features **74**

Other Features **76**

Furniture for your Deck **78**

Lighting your Deck **82**

ADDING A BRIDGE

As well as being used for its traditional purpose of crossing water, a bridge can also be installed as a link between two decks or could even create a short cut across a flower bed. A simple bridge can be built using straight timbers, but why not be more adventurous and build a visually more exciting arched construction to make a real focal point?

Building a bridge is the same as building a narrow deck and providing that the span to cross is short, decking joists can be used in the construction. The obvious disadvantage of decking joists is the lack of a curve to produce the small humpback bridge look; these shaped joists are available from specialist timber merchants who can be found in your local directory.

The design should allow for the width of the crossing and an overhang either side for the starting point.

The smallest joists should be at least 150mm by 50mm for a 2m span, with ideally a 90cm overlap onto the land either side of the stream. A larger overlap will be required if the soil is sandy or subject to erosion. Joist spacing should be closer than on a deck – 30cm on centre as a maximum will be strong enough. The treads should be wide enough for people to walk across without the feeling of a tightrope – 60cm is the minimum width, but 90cm will feel more comfortable to walk on. All grooves must go side-to-side across the bridge to ensure a non-slip surface. Extra maintenance to keep the treads clean will be necessary to avoid accidents. Any cleaning compounds used must be safe as they will fall into the waterway.

ABOVE *A simple bridge can create a focal point to draw you to it and creates a convenient link to other parts of the garden.*

RIGHT *The finished bridge allows a short cut to the other side of the garden. The deck offers a step up onto the bridge, which has an added railing for safety purposes.*

1 *Measure out the first side of the deck by laying the joist across the stream to ensure the correct length is cut. This will also give the position of the footings.*

2 *As you would with a deck, build a frame that is the width required for the bridge, ideally no less than 60cm. Use a central joist to add strength to the frame.*

3 *With the frame complete add noggins to prevent wobble – they will also increase the ridigity of the frame. A bridge that moves as you walk across it is not desirable.*

4 *(right) With help lift the frame into position and level both ways. Install two posts as on the decking by digging in and concreting in place. Bolt the posts to the frame with two coach bolts or coach screws per post for added strength. Check for level as you go. The bridge must be level to create a safe walkway. Drainage is not a problem as it is with a deck as the boards are so short that the water will drain away immediately anyway. As in other decks use preservative on all cut surfaces.*

5 *With the other end secured to the posts fix the bridge to the deck by toenailing the frame to the surface, using long screws to go through the deck boards into the joists.*

6 *Fixing the first tread, use a small block to create an even overhang at the front of the bridge. Space each board 5mm apart to allow for movement in the timber.*

7 *Use self-drilling screws on all treads to stop the boards splitting. The last tread may have to be cut to fit. If its width is reduced too much swap it with the next tread in.*

ADDING HANDRAILS

Not all decks need railings, but if required they should be planned for at the beginning of the project. The design may have to be changed to allow firm fixing points or posts moved to stop a clash of fixings. Other factors will need to be considered. These include the effect that the railings will have on the view and what practical purpose they are intended for.

The main reason for incorporating railings into a deck is for safety, but this need not affect the overall aesthetics of the deck. Most railings have to be of a minimum height and distance between the spindles or horizontal rails. It is a good idea to check with your local building regulations for these exact measurements. The rails must perform their number one role, which is the safety of people on the deck; they must be secure and be able to withstand people leaning against them. It is far better to over-design than under-design in this case and some thought must go into the structure and materials used in the construction of the rails.

As with other aspects of the deck there are many options for the type of rails used and the way they are constructed. Most decking suppliers with have at least one rail in their range, probably many more, but you can design and build your own very easily. From simple wooden rails to copper tube or stainless steel wire running between the posts, the choice is endless. On a windy site you may require a wind break, in which case toughened glass could be used to preserve the view. In situations where the view is not important, solid panels are another alternative.

ABOVE *This is an example of one type of ready made rails. They come complete and just need to be painted and installed, with no assembly required.*
RIGHT *The finished bridge with handrail. Simple and effective, the railings complete the project and add safety and security for people crossing.*

1 *Measure out the position of the bolts; stay at least 4 times the diameter of the bolt from the edge of the timber. Use a wood drill to pre-drill the hole for the coach screws.*

2 *Position the upright and secure the bottom coach screw into position with a spanner. Leave a small gap underneath the post to allow water to run away.*

3 *With a level check that the post is upright and secure in position with another coach screw. You might need a hand to hold the post upright.*

4 *(right) Fix more posts at equal distances across the bridge, no further apart than 1.5m, to support the horizontal rails. When this is done, fix a rail across all the posts using a level as you go. Remember it must be secure as people will lean against it – 100mm by 50mm should be the minimum dimensions for the rail. Remember safety first – do not use any mains-powered drills or saws over the water; use either a cordless or hand saw only. Any cut surfaces should be treated away from the water course.*

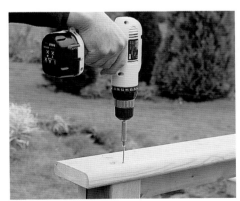

5 *Fix the handrail in place by screwing into the posts rather than the rail. The screws should be twice the thickness of the handrail, to secure it safely.*

6 *Find the centre of the rail between the posts and secure the first one in place, checking to make sure it is upright. With a block of wood as a spacer, secure the top.*

7 *As with the top rail, use the same spacer to create even distances between the posts and secure at the bottom.*

ADDING STEPS

Without doubt almost every deck will need some form of step or stairway. These are easy to build and install, but a few basic rules will make the task simpler. Being outdoors, the steps can be larger and wider, creating a sense of space, and whatever you design they should be inviting to use. Free-flowing steps can lead you around the deck to the garden.

There are three basic methods for building steps. The first is the box method shown opposite. It produces a very simple and strong structure but is best suited for just two or three treads. As the timbers used are normally 100mm or 150mm joists, which are commonly used riser heights for stairs, this makes the box steps easy to work out as the standard timbers do not need to be cut down.

The second method is ideal for a greater amount of steps such as in a stairway between decks and is another simple technique. Two large timbers – known as stringers – 50mm by 250mm or 300mm, can be set between the decks and with stair hangers treads can be screwed between the stringers to produce a stairway. Treads need to be the right width for the riser height.

The last method, cut out stringers, produces the best quality and neatest looking stairs, but requires more working out before you start the job. Cut out stringers are available 'ready to use' but normally cover only three or four steps. You can always purchase a pre-made one and copy the pattern onto a larger piece of timber to increase the length of the stairs. If you have more than three steps a handrail with be required for safety.

LEFT *Posts with ornate tops and patterned panels turn these steps into an attractive feature. How plain or patterned is largely influenced by the style of the building.*

ABOVE *A large flight of steps needs careful planning to ensure safety for the people using it and also to keep it in proportion with the deck and adjacent building.*

1 *When measuring up for the steps, do not have the steps tight between the wall and fence shown here – the steps will expand, moving the fence as well.*

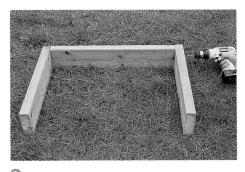

2 *With a tape, measure out the timber, allowing for some movement. Paint all exposed ends with preservative and screw together with framing screws.*

3 *With the base box completed build a second box but reduce the depth by twice the width of the deck board that is to be used as the tread of the step.*

4 *Secure the two boxes together by using offcuts screwed to the inside of the boxes at the back and sides. As before, use framing screws for the fixings.*

5 *Paint any newly cut surfaces with preservative and allow them to dry. This is the last chance to get to this timber before final construction of the steps, so check that all surfaces have been painted. Measure and cut two treads for the lower step. There is no need to leave a space between the boards as on the deck itself.*

6 *With the two treads cut from the decking board, secure in place with two screws at each end to fasten down each one. Cut two more for the top step.*

7 *(left) Level off the base where the steps are to go; you can even use a concrete paving slab if required. Place the steps on the level surface and be sure to check for level again – there is nothing worse than walking up tilting steps. Attach to the main deck with screws.*

8 *(right) The finishing touch for the steps is the top treads. As before, screw down with two screws each end.*

ADDING EDGING

Trim details such as edging are the finishing touches that make a deck complete. The trim should not be seen as an afterthought but an integral part of the design. It should be considered at the beginning of the project as the deck boards will need to finish level with the ends of the joists and frame if they are to accommodate the edging.

Edging covers the ends of the boards to create a finished and professional look to the completed deck. The edging can also be used on the tread of steps as the smooth wood finish stands out more and makes the steps more visible. As well as the aesthetic reasons for the edge, it also stops the ends of the decking boards from splintering if people kick them as they walk up and down the steps. Some decking suppliers produce an edge moulding but a reversed decking board works equally as well, if not better, as the deck board will be thicker and wider than a normal edge moulding. To make the border stand out even more, or to make use of the increased visibility of the smooth edge, the edging can either be stained or painted. As it is not an integral part of the structure it can be removed and replaced quickly and without too much effort.

Edging can also be used between stages of projects by offering a simple disguise for joist posts and other under-deck structures that need to be hidden until the next stage can be started.

ABOVE *This freestanding deck has an edge all round that adds a finished look to the structure.*

RIGHT *The jetty deck with the edge finished and the final screw being fixed at the bridge edge. The trim detail completes the project. The effect of the edging, running from the deck to the bridge, pulls the two projects together via a common thread.*

1 *Measure the length of wood required and cut a board to size. Treat cut ends with preservative and fix in place with screws. Unless you are using self-drilling screws, pre-drill the holes to avoid splitting.*

2 *To infill between the deck and the ground a second board needs to be fixed to the posts for added support. Remember to use a board the same thickness as the joist above, otherwise the infill will not fit .*

3 *Working from the end with the least access, measure and cut boards to fit in a vertical pattern to add interest to the infill. Secure top and bottom with screws. Treat any cut surfaces with preservative.*

4 *In situations where the edging meets soil you can push the bottom of the edging boards into the ground. You can then use a mallet to tap the tops of the boards into place and so create a tight fit.*

5 *(left) The edging can be a specially made edge moulding or, as in this case, a decking board screwed with the grooves facing in. This will produce a strong edge and will be easy to replace in the event that the edging is damaged.*

6 *(above) The deck is completed with the addition of the edging and infill. It makes the deck safe for children and animals as they have no access under the deck. An added bonus is that by excluding light under the deck, weed growth is restricted.*

CONTAINERS FOR YOUR DECK

You can grow almost anything in a pot provided it's big enough. Choosing the right plants is very important but the pots you select will also have an effect on the overall picture. One of the advantages of growing in containers is flexibility. Using pot liners allows you to mix and match seasonal colour and you can move displays around if you feel like a change.

Dressing your deck is always more successful when you go with one particular style. Consider the scale of the decked area and buy pots accordingly. Small pots scattered over a wide expanse of boarding will seem lost and insignificant. The structure should be strong enough to take the weight of one or two large containers and these will help to 'anchor' collections of smaller pots and planters.

Make use of seasonal flowers including annuals, tender perennials and bulbs and when going for a bold display or a more contemporary look, use just one variety per pot rather than a mixture. Pots can be heavy to move around so use a plastic pot as a 'liner'

LEFT *You can easily match wooden containers to the deck especially when they are built into the overall design, e.g. a trough with a trellis backdrop.*

ABOVE *Interesting effects can be created using recessed planters, flush with the deck or by slotting containers into specially shaped apertures.*

and replace these inner sleeves with a fresh display when the original begins to look a bit tired. Wicker baskets painted with yacht varnish to prolong their life make attractive outer covers.

A backdrop of potted evergreens, flowering and foliage shrubs and well-behaved perennials will give continuity of display and give the deck a 'garden' feel. For long-term planting use a well-drained potting mix based on loam and containing a slow-release fertiliser.

For height use small ornamental trees or for a more formal look, shrubs trained as ball-headed standards. Alternatively grow climbers over cane wigwams, metal spirals or obelisks.

CHOOSING YOUR POTS

Terracotta Ranging from classical to contemporary, even rustic. Weathers over time and can be painted with specialist products. Avoid pots with

cracks or flaking and buy guaranteed frost-proof. In cold climates wrap planted pots that can't be moved under cover with layers of insulating material.

Glazed ceramic These come in all shades. Enhance the oriental flavour of pots glazed blue or jade green by surrounding with 'streams' of differently graded cobbles and pebbles. Or for urban chic, try coloured glass beads.

Plastic More expensive examples make quite convincing stone or terracotta look-alikes. Applying artist's acrylic paints can help to 'age' the pots. Perfect where weight is an issue.

Metallic Lightweight containers. Try a row of identical containers planted with grasses or soft-coloured herbs for a more muted display.

Wood Leave natural and treat with preservative (plastic inner liners help lengthen their life further) or paint an appropriate colour.

ABOVE LEFT *Marguerite daisies look fresh and contemporary in blue glazed pots.*
ABOVE RIGHT *Hydrangeas make surprisingly good pot specimens but need plenty of moisture and a little shade.*
BELOW *The clean lines of today's galvanized, zinc or aluminium containers make them a must for contemporary gardens. Miniature bamboo is used here to stylish effect.*

PLANTS FOR YOUR DECK

Whilst more or less anything goes in gardens today, certain styles of planting seem to work particularly well with decking. The crisp, clean lines of these solid wooden structures often confer a markedly 'architectural' feel that looks even more impressive combined with bold, sculpted flowers and foliage as well as ornamental grasses and bamboos.

You can plant directly on the deck using all manner of containers but for larger elements such as trees and vigorous climbers, it makes more sense to plant through the deck so that the root system has access to a much greater volume of soil. This really needs to be thought about at the construction stage since it is much more convenient to plant a large specimen first and build the deck around it. As well as the purely practical advantages, planting through specially shaped apertures in the deck can produce very stylish results, especially when bands of identical plants are used. If the deck is too far off the ground, consider using recessed planters flush with the floor level to produce a similar effect.

USE YOUR IMAGINATION

A deck can be thought of as a raised viewing platform providing a different perspective on the garden and its plants. By surrounding it with lush plantings you could create the illusion of a floating raft surrounded by water regardless of whether the ground is naturally damp.

The trick is to be bold. Plant dramatic swathes of taller ornamental grasses and plants with grass-like leaves such as *Iris sibirica*, *crocosmia* and daylily (*Hemerocallis*). Contrast these with broad-leaf perennials including hostas and bergenias. You can also try out large ferns such as *Dryopteris filix-mas* and ferny-leaved plants like the statuesque goat's beard (*Aruncus dioicus*). These plants all suggest moisture, yet are perfectly happy growing on any good garden soil.

OPPOSITE *The herbs in this built-in container set close to the house are ideally placed for kitchen access. You could also grow a mixture of salad crops or strawberries*
RIGHT *A variegated phormium provides a strong vertical accent that contrasts well with the horizontal lines of decking and is impressive enough to stand alone.*
BELOW *Hi-tech metal spirals are used in place of more traditional wooden trellis to give support for climbers – here golden hop (Humulus lupulus 'Aureus').*

ABOVE *For the greatest impact, plant seasonal flowers like this vibrant petunia as single specimens. Planting identical pots in a row is especially dramatic.*
ABOVE RIGHT *The delicate foliage of Japanese maples contrasts beautifully with broad-leaved evergreens. Provide shelter from strong sunlight and wind and keep well watered.*
OPPOSITE *Large ferns make wonderful specimens for shade. Grow them in pots or in borders surrounding the deck with other shade lovers like hostas, ornamental sedges and bamboos. Ferns also look good in an oriental setting, perhaps with a mulch of rounded cobbles and pebbles.*

DIVERSE PLANTS

A bog garden adjacent to your deck allows for even more luxuriant planting. Simply line a shallow depression with pond liner punctured a few times to allow excess water to drain away, then backfill with compost-enriched soil and give the whole area a thorough soaking. You can then grow one of the most spectacular of all garden plants, *Gunnera manicata*, as well as the sculptural rheums and rodgersias, the royal fern (*Osmunda regalis*) and ferny-leaved astilbes and filipendulas.

In a sheltered city garden you could let your imagination run riot and give your deck a jungle feel. For a subtropical flavour you could use any of the above-mentioned foliage plants, choosing ones with scarlet, orange or white flowers. Then add other 'exotica' including graceful clump-forming bamboos (forms of *Phyllostachys* and *Fargesia* are generally problem free), glossy-leaved *Fatsia japonica* and New Zealand flax (*Phormium*).

Hardy palms like *Trachycarpos fortunei* strengthen the illusion of gardening in a hot climate and certain small ornamental trees also have the right look. Try the sumach (*Rhus typhina*), the gold-leaved *Robinia pseudoacacia* 'Frisia' or the golden form of the Indian bean tree (*Catalpa bignonioides* 'Aurea').

EASTERN INFLUENCES

Although a shady aspect is not ideal for decks because of slippery algae, a deck sheltered from strong sunlight could

ABOVE *A standard bay tree planted in a galvanized container and set against a sunny whitewashed wall gives this deck a contemporary feel.*

RIGHT *When planting on and around a deck it pays to be bold. Here a swathe of white marguerite daisies makes a classic statement.*

OPPOSITE *Make a dramatic entrance by planting identical containers with architectural plants like* Fatsia japonica *(pictured) or perhaps a pair of neatly clipped topiary spirals or elegant ball-headed standards. These large square trellis planters are ideal for permanent plantings including climbers that need a large soil volume.*

become the central focus of a restful Japanese-inspired planting. In Japan it is quite common for wooden verandas (a type of decking) to be surrounded by gravel and stepping stones.

To enhance the atmosphere you could introduce a bubbling water feature set into the deck surrounded by pebbles and cobbles and hang wind chimes from an overhead pergola. Plant the surrounds with mainly cool green foliage, varying the leaf texture and shading as much as possible. Shrubs including acid-loving red- or white-flowered camellias, rhododendrons and azaleas, as well as white or blue lace-cap hydrangeas, will provide the odd touch of colour, but the emphasis is on foliage – try combining plants like ferns, hostas, spotted laurel (*Aucuba japonica*), Japanese maples, bamboos, ornamental grasses and sedges.

MEDITERRANEAN FEEL

In a hot, sunny spot, decking combined with gravel also allows for a more Mediterranean style of planting with drought-resistant types such as many of the 'silverlings' like carpeting lamb's ears (*Stachys byzantina*), white daisy-flowered Rhodanthemum hosmariense and lacey artemisias. Use plenty of herbs and aromatic plants like catmints (*Nepeta sp.*), lavenders, thymes, sages, bronze fennel and oregano to create soft drifts that will contrast pleasingly with the stronger lines of the decking.

Then introduce a few architectural plants including perennials like *Acanthus spinosus* and verbascum as well as yuccas, phormiums or astelias, the latter with their metallic sword-shaped leaves. Pots of brightly coloured geraniums and succulents would provide the perfect finishing touch.

WATER FEATURES

The sight and sound of moving water literally brings the garden to life. And even a still pool
generates a special atmosphere with the changing reflections and all the bird and insect life
it attracts. Decks offer wonderful opportunities for creating stylish and innovative water
features that range from simple self-contained fountains to pools, rills and cascades.

Ready-made kits to construct water features take very little time or skill to install provided you have a convenient electricity supply, though buying the various elements individually may be cheaper and allow greater flexibility of design. Fountains with a hidden

reservoir have several advantages. They are child-safe; they don't need cleaning out like conventional ponds; and there is very little labour involved in their construction. When planning the location of your water feature, try and avoid exposed areas where the wind

might blow the fountain jet out of position. Left unchecked, this could quickly empty the reservoir and there is always the chance that it might damage the pump.

When building a pool set into the deck, you may be able to avoid any

OPPOSITE LEFT *A wooden half-barrel makes an ideal pool for a small deck. Remember to put it in position before you fill it up!*
OPPOSITE RIGHT *The composition of this self-contained fountain and the two polished spheres is superbly balanced.*
ABOVE LEFT *Some little bubble fountains are like modern sculptures. This one has its own water reservoir so just needs plugging in.*
ABOVE RIGHT *Gleaming pebbles splashed by a bell fountain make an eye-catching feature. The reservoir and pump are under the deck, covered with rigid wire mesh.*

WATER SAFETY

If in any doubt, hire a qualified electrician to install electrical water features such as pumps and lighting. Use waterproof fittings and connect to a residual current device (RCD) or circuit breaker. Avoid having any depth of water exposed where young children are around.

excavations – just use a black, pre-formed liner, properly supported, and overlap the planks slightly to hide the edges. A raised pool with a wooden seat going all the way around it is another attractive option, providing a lovely area for socializing with a few friends or contemplating on your own. Square or rectangular-shaped pools look good with the rectilinear layout of most decks, but a circle or semi-circle at the base of a wall mask fountain can also be very striking.

PREPARING THE WATER

The water in your feature will keep clean and clear once you have established some submerged aquatics as oxygenators. A pump connected to a filter will also help to prevent a shallow pool from becoming stagnant. Leave the bottom of the pool clear to create maximum reflection.

Choose your water plants carefully as many are overly vigorous and could rapidly swamp a small pool. Luckily, you can buy miniature water lilies that will flower in something as small as a wooden half-barrel. Be aware that fish need a depth of at least 90cm (3ft) in part of the pool as protection from winter cold. Have the quality and pH of the water tested by your aquatic centre before introduction. If any part of wooden decking comes into contact with the water, ensure that it has not been treated with harmful preservatives that could pollute.

When a deck is split between different levels you have the option of building a series of pools linked by gentle cascades. However, it is vital that you check what power and type of pump you require with your supplier otherwise you might be disappointed at the speed and volume of output.

OTHER FEATURES

Before you settle on a final layout for your deck, it pays to spend some time thinking about the finishing touches. These might be practical or decorative. Ask yourself who will be using the deck – children and older people need careful consideration. Also ask how it will be used – for dining al fresco, sitting out in the evenings, or as a children's play area?

Decks are often built on the side of a house or round a garden building, creating an extension of the living space. The impression of an outdoor room can be strengthened by linking the deck and building via some kind of overhead structure to form a 'ceiling'. Simple wooden pergolas fulfil this function admirably. If the deck is in a hot, sunny spot, the pergolas can be adapted to provide a little shade or offer a certain degree of seclusion.

Wooden pergolas can be bought off the peg from DIY stores and builder's merchants but you can also get your local timber yard to cut the necessary pieces to your own specifications. Getting the proportions right is the key to success. The uprights need to have substance and the height of the structure and spacing of the components should create a feeling of spaciousness not claustrophobia!

Plan it on paper and then stick to your guns. It may well look too big at first, but when covered with climbers it will blend in nicely. Don't forget to make provision for the plants,

ABOVE *A standalone feature such as this angled trellis screen and planter could be positioned to give height and a little privacy.*

LEFT *A large expanse of deck might seem quite stark at first but a pergola can instantly make the space feel comfortable. A nice design touch here is that the central uprights are set within the deck. Plant a vigorous climber such as a rambler rose, Clematis montana or a vine to quickly soften the structure.*

OPPOSITE *The tree that this deck was built around is a real focal point. Its importance has been further emphasized by the hexagonal seat, painted blue to contrast with the natural coloured decking.*

ABOVE *Gas-powered patio heaters extend the use of the deck when it would normally be too cold to sit out.*

BELOW *If the deck is to be used by small children, safety is of the utmost importance. Building a sand pit in one corner of the deck, perhaps backed by trellis panels, will help to confine the play area and make it easier to supervise.*

preparing the ground and planting holes before the deck is laid.

Once the basic framework is up, you can add decorative features such as specially shaped trellis elements. Interesting effects of light and shade can be achieved by laying patterned trellis panels over the crossbeams. For an oriental look or for maximum privacy or shelter from wind, consider fitting bamboo, heather or wicker panels between the uprights. Square-pattern trellis fencing panels create a feeling of enclosure and security but the deck still feels light and airy.

CHILD-FRIENDLY

Built-in planters and furniture such as bench seating can really make a feature on the deck, especially when picked out in a contrasting or complementary shade. Waterproof wooden lockers can also be incorporated, perhaps within a seating unit, to store cushions and toys for easy access. Small children will love to play out on the deck and a sand pit could become a focus for their games. Match the timber and construction style and build a waterproof cover to keep the sand clean and dry when not in use.

FURNITURE FOR YOUR DECK

Garden furniture can be purely functional like a wooden picnic table. But there are some beautiful designs around today that add greatly to the garden scene because they have such a pleasing form. Shop around to find chairs and tables that are both practical and capable of enhancing the view from the house, selecting furniture that fits into your overall scheme.

Chairs and tables can be expensive but there are designs to suit any budget and taste and you can always substitute cheaper furniture elements while you save up for what you really want. Consider practicality, comfort, style, longevity, maintenance and price. Also think about whether or not you intend to leave chairs and tables out through the winter. If not, how you will store them? Waterproof covers are available for protecting furniture sets out of season but these are unsightly and could spoil the view from the house. Always check that wooden furniture comes from a sustainable source, especially when dealing with tropical hardwoods. It is especially important to avoid mahogany, as this is an endangered species.

VERSATILE WOOD

Having permanent seating on the deck is an enticement to sit out when the weather is fine. Wood is ideal for this because it dries off quite quickly after a shower and is warm and comfortable to sit on without the need for cushions. Wooden furniture is an obvious partner for decking. If your deck has been coloured, you can paint it to match or

ABOVE *A wooden picnic table creates an informal atmosphere and is ideal for family dining but takes up quite a large space.*
RIGHT *This hi-tech aluminium set would fit into any corner. Combine with metal planters and architectural foliage for a contemporary look but don't forget some cushions – metal is cold to the touch!*

to contrast and if natural, most wood types will blend together with ease.

Treat softwood furniture with preservative to prolong its life – some treatments combine colour with water-repellent agents and chemicals to deter rot. The more expensive hardwoods, including tropical types like iroko, have a much denser grain and are naturally more resistant to fungal attack. Use the recommended furniture oil to soak in, nourish and waterproof the wood. You can also use clear yacht varnish but this needs frequent application.

STYLISH METAL

Some furniture designs combine wooden slats with a metal framework – you can often buy quite reasonably priced fold-away bistro style sets that are easy to store when not in use. Be

aware, however, that unless the metal is galvanized or the framework is made from aluminium, stainless steel or chrome, it will rust. Victorian cast iron bench seat ends or their reproductions are usually painted and some metal furniture is lacquered or coated with plastic to help prevent rust. But as soon as the paint or protective surface is damaged, rusting occurs, leaving unsightly stains on the deck. All-metal furniture sets can be very stylish but

ABOVE *This table and chair set combining wooden slats with a metal frame, gives a light, airy feel to the furniture making it an ideal choice for a small deck.*
LEFT *Bright, stripy deckchairs help to create a relaxed seaside atmosphere to the deck. You could carry the motif further with a heavy rope surround, pebbles and silver- or grey-leaved plants.*

cushions are essential for comfort – metal is very cold on bare legs!

Wood and canvas furniture such as director's chairs are often quite stylish. They have the advantage of being light and easy to move around but must be kept out of the rain. A waterproof locker built into the deck will make for quick access and is also perfect for storing floor cushions. Striped canvas deckchairs are fun and are usually very cheap to buy but can be tricky to erect.

Finally, if you don't have a leafy pergola to shelter under during the heat of the day, you'll need some kind of canvas umbrella or awning. Sun parasols come in all sizes, colours and designs to suit any budget and either fit through a hole in the centre of the table or are self-supporting. Awnings can be traditional rectangles of canvas or, more imaginatively, cut like sails that are winched out to cover varying amounts of the deck as required.

ABOVE *The Italian styling of this smart table and chairs set adds a note of distinction. Cushion pads would make the seating more comfortable and an umbrella would give welcome shade on a hot day.*
LEFT *Outdoor furniture as beautiful as this reproduction steamer chair provides a strong incentive to sit out on the deck and enjoy the garden.*
RIGHT *Hardwood furniture can be the most expensive type to buy but, with its up-market looks and excellent durability, it is a good investment.*

LIGHTING YOUR DECK

Once you've completed your new deck, you'll want to spend as much time as possible enjoying it. Quite apart from the safety aspect of illuminating steps and changes in level, lighting will dramatically extend the use of the deck and can create a magical ambience. Even when it's too cold to be outside, you can still enjoy the view through the windows at night.

A little planning at the design and construction stage of your deck will not only make installation easier but also ensure that unsightly wiring is hidden away. Try to build in some flexibility so that through the evening you have the option to change the lighting to suit your mood. Avoid reliance on powerful halogen security lights.

The range of outdoor light fittings available direct to the amateur from shops is fairly limited but mail order companies offer a wide choice. The majority run off mains electricity and unless you have experience of fitting outdoor electrical appliances, it may be wise to call in a professional.

MAINS ELECTRICITY

The effect of black mini-spot uplighters and downlighters is quite subtle and they are particularly useful for

LEFT *The flickering light of garden candles and lanterns adds a touch of magic to the deck. Place around sitting areas, to softly illuminate a dining table, amongst the foliage of plants and to highlight a water feature – imagine candles reflected in a still pool at night! Take extra care with candles on a wooden deck.*

highlighting decorative trellis, ornaments, water features and plants. Dress trellis panels and climber-covered pergolas with tiny white fairy lights – lovely for creating a romantic atmosphere for an outdoor dining area. Another soft lighting technique uses recessed lights that are flush with the deck and safe to walk over. Their metal finishes offer a contemporary feel.

Ideal around doorways, there are several designs of wall light including those that match the period detailing of your house. You can connect these to an infra-red sensor so that the lights come on automatically when it gets dark. Use long-life bulbs where possible and, for safety's sake, connect to a residual current device (RCD) or circuit breaker.

LOW-VOLTAGE LIGHTING

Low-voltage lights running off a transformer are easy for the amateur to install. The range is fairly limited – you normally buy a set of four or eight identical lights, e.g. spotlights on spikes to push into the ground or pots, globe lamps on a stem, or lights set into a column. Some come with sensors that switch them on automatically at night.

Solar-powered lights have come on in leaps and bounds and better brands now function quite reliably even in dull weather thanks to advances in re-chargeable battery technology. They are similar in design to those that run off a transformer but have the advantage of being wireless, so can operate far away from an electricity supply.

Candle lanterns, garden candelabras and flares now come in a wealth of designs and are perfect for warm summer nights when eating outdoors. Choose from opulent, high-tech or rustic. Set them amongst the plants, floating on your pool, hanging from the pergola or at the centre of the table. But don't leave naked flames unattended!

ABOVE *Exterior wall lights come in a range of styles from traditional to modern like this contemporary coloured glass lamp. Wall lights are good for highlighting doorways.*
BELOW LEFT *Mains electric lamps can provide unobtrusive low-level lighting for decks.*
BELOW CENTRE *This elegant Japanese-style lantern operates via solar-powered batteries so there are no wires to conceal and you can move the light wherever you need it.*
BELOW RIGHT *Modern downlighters such as these are available mains-powered, as low-voltage lighting sets or as independent solar-powered units.*

CHAPTER FOUR

HELP!

Maintaining your Deck   86

Re-finishing your Deck   88

Suppliers List   90

Acknowledgements   91

Index   92

MAINTAINING YOUR DECK

As with any outdoor surface, there are routine tasks to be carried out on your deck to ensure that it stays looking smart. Most of the work is quick and easy provided you do it fairly regularly and tackle potential problems sooner rather than later. Remember that wood is a living material that will reward you with its beauty if you take the trouble to look after it well.

It pays to go over the deck with a fine-tooth comb at the start of the season, looking for any damage that might have occurred over winter such as loosened boards. Then give the deck a thorough clean. Begin by clearing off ornaments, pots and pieces of furniture and using a stout yard broom, sweep away all the dead leaves and other litter, moss and soil, working carefully along the grooves to help prevent debris from falling between the planks.

Sweeping the dirt *Sweep dirt along the grooves to stop it from falling between the deck boards (below). If dirt or other types of material have fallen underneath the deck, a powerful wet and dry vacuum can be used to extract it.*

ALGAE AND STAIN REMOVAL
Particularly in a shady spot, algae and moss may have built up due to autumn and winter dampness and this should be removed using a stiff hand brush and a strong antifungal wash or garden disinfectant designed for the purpose. If the problem is severe and the deck has become slippery as a result, it may be necessary to cover the worst affected areas with galvanized chicken wire mesh, firmly tacked down to provide extra grip underfoot. Next to a building check the state of the guttering or overflow pipes – water may have been pouring directly down onto the deck over winter.

Tightening the screws *If the deck is laid when the timber is wet, the wood will shrink and the screw heads could then be raised above the surface during the drier months. Tighten the screws down.*

If the deck has become dirty or badly stained, one way to rejuvinate it is to use a high-pressure water sprayer. You can hire these, but they are only suitable for decks that have not been painted with a surface treatment. The jet is very powerful and may lift off paint or varnish. Rust marks from furniture can be especially hard to shift and if the sprayer doesn't work, you may have to resort to using a chemical rust remover or a sander to lift off the top layer.

STRUCTURAL WORK

Before the deck comes into regular use, check that the support structure is still sound and that there are no rotting timbers. In rural areas check that burrowing animals have not undermined the supports and block off their access if this has occurred.

Wood expands and contracts with changes in moisture levels and if the deck was laid when the timber was wet, when it dries out in summer, you may find that the screws have loosened. Tighten up with a power screwdriver.

If some of the deck has been badly damaged, remove the affected boards and replace or cut out the affected area and piece in with matching material.

OTHER TASKS

If you did not cover the soil beneath the deck at the outset, then weed growth may be a problem. Weeds look unsightly sticking through the cracks but reaching their roots can be tricky in a restricted space. Spray protruding leaves with a systemic weed-killer.

Surface treatments will need to be re-applied before they start to look worn and shabby. It's much easier to apply a quick coat to spruce up an existing treatment than to prepare the wood from scratch.

DECK CLEANING SCHEDULE

Once a week Sweep deck to remove all leaves and debris from the surface.

Once a month Remove any weeds or plants growing between boards or out from under the deck.

In the autumn Wash down deck with a good algaecide/moss inhibitor.

Ready for winter Protect all pots from frost.

Once a year Wash down deck and remove furniture and ornaments. Repair if necessary and re-finish if required.

Splinters *If the decking is damaged or splinters are seen, cut the splinter off with a utility knife and then sand with the grain until the surface is smooth again. Use a block to keep the sandpaper flat.*

Antifungal wash *All timber will attract algae and mould. In the autumn a wash down with a antifungus/mould and algae killer will help to reduce the growth that can be very slippery in wet weather.*

Damaged boards. *If the deck surface is damaged, it should be relatively easy to replace the boards. Unscrew the board and either replace the whole length or, as here, cut the board and replace a section.*

RE-FINISHING YOUR DECK

As in interior design, the colour of the moment can change from year to year. When finishing your deck remember it will take many hours of work to change the colour if you decide it's not in fashion any more, so choose the colour carefully. A simple stained oil or clear preservative is often the best choice and easy to reapply every year.

As with other aspects of the deck you have a choice that is almost endless. The important factors to consider are the type of wood, the deck's designed use and the amount of traffic across it; all these will affect the type of finish you should use. If the deck is in an exposed position a long-lasting finish will be required to prevent excess weathering. Even if the weathered look is preferred, a clear sealant will have to be used on less expensive woods. However, with high quality, pressure-treated timber the weathered look can be realized by simply leaving the timber alone.

The final colour of the deck will vary depending on different timber species and the strength of sunlight. In time most timbers will lighten to an ash grey. If the 'just built' look is desired, apply a coloured stain to the timber – it will need to be reapplied each year since the colour will wear off with use.

The other option is to paint the deck. This will completely cover the underlying wood so is an ideal finish if you are using a budget timber. Although painting takes longer it is easy to apply and areas of deck that will be difficult to reach can be painted before assembly. On the deck's surface you will have to make sure the finish will be slip-resistant. For this and advice on the paint to use, speak to a paint specialist.

STAINING THE DECK

There are two basic stains you can apply to the deck. The first is a semi-transparent or low-pigmented stain which will show the wood to its best effect but will require more frequent restaining. The second is a solid or heavy pigmented stain, which is best if wood defects need to be hidden. It is longer lasting and easier to apply, so a good choice for lower grade timber.

BEFORE YOU PAINT

Before you rush out and buy the paint consider the following:
• **The deck will have to be re-painted every year.**
• **Heavy wear can make painted surfaces look shabby very quickly.**
• **It's very difficult to remove the paint or stain once it's been applied.**
• **A strong, non-neutral deck shade may restrict your ability to try different colour schemes.**

Re-varnishing *With the deck cleaned and swept, remove all the loose varnish. Depending on the varnish you may need to sand the surface to get a better key. Then paint on the required number of coats.*

Disguise beams *This is to make the ends of beams and joists less of an eyesore. Paint the ends with a dark colour to make them less obvious. Make sure the paint can cover the preservative used on the timber.*

Re-painting the deck *As decks weather it may be necessary to repaint the surface. Use a good quality outdoor timber paint or coloured preservative, and follow the recommendations for application.*

SUPPLIERS LIST

The publishers wish to thank the following suppliers who kindly lent props and photographs to include in the book. Listed after each entry are the details of any props used. Following this are the credits for the pictures, where the following key is used: t = top, l = left, r = right, c = centre, b = bottom. All other photos by Neil Sutherland.

ARCADIAN GARDEN FEATURES LIMITED

The Forge House
East Haddon
Northampton NN6 8DB
Tel: 01604 770020
Fax: 01604 770027
Email: info@haddonstone.co.uk
Web: www.arcadiangf.co.uk
Crucible fountain GC200 pp.35, 74 br,
Eclipse fountain GC230 pp.9, 46-47, 56, 75, 79 b.
Arcadian garden table GD650 pp.30-31, 80 t

ARCHADECK

The Old Shipyard
Gainsborough
Lincolnshire DN21 1NG
Tel: 0800 783 2909
Web: www.archadeck.co.uk
Custom designs from the world's leading turn-key deck construction company. Call the above number for a free brochure.
The following photograph: p.62 r

ARUN LANDSCAPES

Sloe Cottage
Northstoke
Arundel
West Sussex BN18 9LS
Tel/Fax: 01798 831045
Email: madaline@btinternet.com
Web: www.arunlandscapes.co.uk
All the projects were built by the team at Arun Landscapes: Nick Ralph, Steve Dalmon, Matthew and Frank Tilbury.

DECKSDIRECT LTD

Brooke House
Market Square
Aylesbury
Bucks HP20 1SN
Tel: 01296 718620
Fax: 01296 718621
Web: www.decksdirect.co.uk
Email: decksdirect@aol.com
DecksDirect offer nationwide comprehensive deck design and construction services to the domestic and commercial marketplaces. Call us to request your free brochure and to arrange your free design consultation.
The following photographs: pp.54-55

DIG-IT

Mail order style solutions for your garden. Our inspiration for your garden covers carefully chosen decorative features, lights, furniture and tools to exciting collections of plants chosen by our experts. Call 0870 120 1360 for a catalogue or buy online at www.dig-it.co.uk
Hardwood furniture set pp.50-51, 70, 81
Party lights p.83 br
Kyoto hanging solar lantern p.83 bc
Helix patio heater p.77 tr
Metalic silver globes pp.7, 34-35,
Galvanized container pp.35, 67 br,
Galvanized bucket pp.38,

FINNFOREST UK

FinnForest UK are suppliers of Garden Decking and many other wood-based products, to the merchant and DIY market. For further information about FinnForest or a list of our stockists, please phone 0800 004444 or consult www.finnforest.co.uk.
All the projects were built with decking kindly supplied by FinnForest.

FOREST GARDEN

Stanford Court
Stanford Bridge
Worcester WR6 6SR
Tel: 01886 811030
Fax: 01886 812348
Email: info@forestgarden.co.uk
Web: www.forestgarden.co.uk
Forest Garden is the UK's largest manufacturer of timber products for the garden. From arches to arbours, decking to decorative trellis, planters to pergolas, Forest Garden has a product to suit your tastes and requirements. Phone the above number for a free 48-page colour brochure.
Chelsea Planters pp.6, 17 tr, 72,
Oxford Corner Planter pp.39, 47, 68,
York (hexagonal) Planters pp.6, 17 tr, 42-43, 47,
Madrid Planter (with trelis) pp.6, 17, 42-43, 72 b,
Pebble Fountain pp.19, 39, 75 r,
And the following photographs: pp.11, 22 l, 23 tl, 23 tc, 23 tr, 23 bl, 58 l, 60 l, p62 l, 76 bl, 76tr, 88

HADDONCRAFT FORGE

The Forge House
East Haddon
Northampton NN6 8DB
Tel: 01604 580559
Fax: 01604 580541
Email: info@haddonstone.co.uk
Web: www.haddoncraft.co.uk
Haddoncraft Harleston Chair WD500 pp.30-31, 80

HILLHOUT

Hillhout Limited
Unit 18, Elough Industrial Estate
Beccles
Suffolk NR34 7TD
Tel: 01502 718091
Fax: 01502 718082
Web: www.hillhout.com
Hillhout has been manufacturing quality wooded garden products for some 30 years. Everything you might need, from cabins, decking, pergolas to fencing and furniture. Contact us on the above number for a brochure.
Bistro table and chairs pp.6, 17 tr, 42-43, 79 tr,
Excellent Planter pp.19, 39, 66 l,
And the following photographs: pp10 l, 22 r, 23 br, 76 tl, 76 br, 78 bl, 83 bl,

JARDINAIRE

Thomas Telford House
1 Heron Quay
London E14 4JD
Tel: 00 44 207 538 9373
Fax: 00 44 207 515 1447
Web: www.jardinaire.com
Jardinaire's unique light sculptures provide dramatic outdoor lighting features combining form and function to provide a focal centrepiece for outdoor lighting schemes. The Luminessence range, which includes the tri-lights, can be used indoors and in close vicinity to water, i.e. bathrooms, showers and pools.
Tri-light p.83 tr

RICHARD BURBIDGE

Whittington Road
Oswestry
Shropshire SY11 1HZ
Tel: 01691 678201
Email: infoa@richardburbidge.co.uk
Web: www.richardburbidge.co.uk
Manufacturers of decorative timber products. An extensive range of decking products, full systems, deck boards, joists, fixings and innovative, stylish balustrading. Phone the above number for a brochure or visit our website, where a comprehensive guide to decking and a 'how to' video are available to order.
The following photographs: pp.10 r, 12, 80 b, 82,

SCREWFIX DIRECT

The UK's premier mail-order supplier of tools fixings, building supplies and power tools for trade and DIY. Call 0500 414141 for a catalogue or buy online at www.screwfix.com
DeWalt Compound saw p26

THE AUTHOR WOULD LIKE TO THANK...

FinnForest for supplying the timber used in all the projects.
The men from Arun Landscapes who built the decks: Nick Ralph, Steve Dalmon, Matthew and Frank Tilbury. The home owners that allowed us to use their gardens: Tracy Musson and Mike Rusby for the Raised and Freestanding decks; Dawn and Steve Barnard-Voice for the Split-level Deck; and Colin Walton and Jonathan Flett for the Simple Square deck, Angled Deck with Access Panels and the Jetty Deck.

INDEX

This index lists all the projects, building instructions and techniques mentioned in the book. It also comprises entries for essential tools, materials and important ancillary information. For a general guide to the book, see the list of contents on page 9. Page numbers in *italic* refer to illustrations.

A
access panels 36-7, 41
air bricks 40, 42, 44, 45
algae 17, 38, 71, 86, *87*
angled deck 34-7
awnings 80

B
balconies 22, 55
bamboo *67*, 71
battens 22
beams 13, *20*
  disguising ends 89
  for jetty deck 50, 52
boards *20*
  damaged 87
  finishes 20
  fixing 33
  reversed, as edger 64
  widths 18
bog garden 71
bolts 21
box-method steps 62, 63
bridges *50*, 58-9
building regulations 54, 55, 60

C
candles and lanterns *82*
cantilever deck 50-3
cascades 75
chicken wire mesh 86

children 77
cleaning 86, *86*, 87
climbers 67, 68, *69*, 76
cobbles 67, *71*, 72
concrete blocks 38, 63
  cutting 27
construction adhesive 52
containers 66-7, *69*, *71-3*
  built-in 46, *68*, 77
  recessed *66*, 68
cut out stringers 62

D
damp course 38, 46
deckchairs *79*, 80
decking squares 22
delivery 25
design 16-18, 55, 60
designer, choosing 55
diagonal boards, laying 40
director's chairs 80
drainage 23, 24-5, 59
drains and drainpipes 24, 86
  building round 34, 36-7

E
edgings *20*, 64-5
electrics 17, 75, 82-3
estimating quantities 19

F
fairy lights 83
fences 18, 42, 45, 63
ferns 68, *70*, 71
finishing 88-9
fish 75
fixings 21
flowers 66, *67*, 71, *71*, *72*
foliage 67, 68, 69, 71-2
footings 13, 25
fountains 74, *74*, 75
freestanding deck 46-9

G
grasses, ornamental 68
gravel 24, 72
grooved boards 17, 21

H
hand rails *11*, 17, *20*, 42
  adding 60-1
  bridges *58*, 60
  stairs 62
herbs *68*, 72
hole saw 37
humpback bridge 58

J
Japanese style 71-2, 77, *83*
jetty deck 50-3
joints 18-19

joists 13, 23
  for bridge 58
  curved 58
  fixing 32
  for jetty deck 50, 52

L

lawn, protecting 25
ledger board 13, 30, 32
low-voltage lighting 83

M

maintenance 17, 58, 86-7
manhole covers 34, 36-7, 41
marking techniques 27
Mediterranean-style 72
metal furniture *78*, 79-80, *80*
modular decking 22

N

nails 21
noggins 13, 33

P

painting 89
parasols 80
paths and walkways *10*, *22*, 55
patio, building over 22, 24-5, 34
patio heaters 77
patterns *11*, 18, *23*, *38*
pebbles 67, *71*, 72, *75*
pergolas 76-7, *76*
piers 25, 52
planning 16-19, 54, *62*, 74, 76, 82
planning permission 19, 55
plans, drawing *18*, 19
planters, see containers
plants 66-72
  incorporating 42, 44-5, 68
  removing from site 24
  trimming back 25

pools and ponds *54*, 74-5
  overhanging deck 50-3
posts 13, *20*, 40, *62*
pot liners 66-7
pots, types 67
power tools 26, 27, 50, 53
privacy 17, 42, *76*, 77
professionals 17, 54-5, 75

R

railings, see handrails
raised-level deck 42-5
ready-made decking 22-3
ready-made rails *60*
recessed lights 83
roof decks 22
rust marks 87

S

safety 17, 27, 50, 60, 62, 75
sand pit 77, *77*
sawing techniques 27
saws 26
screwing angled timber 48
screws 21
  tightening *86*, 87
sealant 27, 63, 89
seats 78-80
  permanent 77, *77*, 78
shade 17, 18, 42, 76
  plants for 71-2, *71*
shrubs 67, 72
site, choosing 16
skip hire 25
sleepers 22
slopes *16*, 30, 42, 46
softwood 20, 79
soil 24, 25, 38
  types 22, 58
spacer 33
splinters 87

split-level deck 38-41
square deck 30-4
square, checking for 48, 52
stain removal 87
stairs and steps 13, 17, 18,
  21, 55, 62-3
storage space 77, 80
stringers 62
structural repairs 87
subtropical plants 71
sun 17, 42, 72

T

tanalized timber 17, 20, 27
terms, decking 13
timber 20
  storing 25
tool hire 26
treads 58, 62, 63, 64
trees 67, 68, 71, *71*, 72
  removing stumps 24
trellis 42, 46, *76*, 77

U

up- and downlighters 82-3, *83*

V

varnish 89

W

wall lights 83, *83*
warped boards 33
water features 72, 74-5
water plants 75
weathered look 89
weeds 23, 24, 25, 36, 65, 87
wicker baskets 67
wind breaks 17, 60, 77
wood stain 89
wooden containers *66*, 67
wooden furniture 78-9, *78*